Cap.

By the same author

Foreign Investments in India
Pakistan's Trade With Eastern Bloc Countries
Economic Development in South Asia (with E.A.G. Robinson)
Western Capitalism Since the War

Michael Kidron

CAPITALISM AND THEORY

Pluto  Press

First published 1974
by Pluto Press Limited
Unit 10, Spencer Court
7 Chalcot Road, London NW1 8LH

ISBN 0 902818 47 3 paperback
ISBN 0 902818 48 1 hardback

Printed by
The Camelot Press Limited
Southampton

Designed by
Richard Hollis, GrR

Preface

These essays are about the permanent arms economy – the latest, final phase of capitalism – and about the body of theory that can make sense of it – marxism. They have a common purpose – to weaken the system and to strengthen the analysis while underlining the unity of the two.

The essays that form the core of the book – 'Waste: US 1970' written in collaboration with Elana Gluckstein, and 'Black Reformism' written with help from her and Dennis Childs – are published here for the first time. The others have appeared before but have been *raubdrucked* often enough to suggest that they are still live. Except for obvious typographical errors, they are presented here exactly as first published, with all their imperfections. 'Capitalism – the Latest Stage' appeared in *World Crisis, Essays in Revolutionary Socialism,* edited by Nigel Harris and John Palmer, London: Hutchinson, 1971; Chapters 3, 4, 6 and 7, were first published in *International Socialism* no.32, 1968, no.36, 1969, no.9, 1962, and no.20, 1965. 'Memories of Development' was first printed in *New Society*, 4 March 1971.

London
March 1974

Contents

8

Part Two: Centre and Periphery

Introduction

1. Capitalism: the Latest Stage

I.

Introduction

A hundred or a hundred and fifty years ago capitalism was a fairly small system contained within a few nation states. Few ruling classes saw survival in terms of the accumulation of capital. Now even the most powerful states are no more than components of the system; and only a handful of ruling classes can escape the compulsion to increase productive capacity endlessly.

Individual capitals have grown immensely from small and insecure beginnings through amalgamation, absorption and destruction. They are now so huge as to sometimes constitute a single state capital as happens in the East. And even where they are smaller, as in the West, they have become large enough to make co-ordination amongst themselves and between them and their states both possible and necessary. Planning of a sort has invaded the nation state, and sometimes even transcends it.

Relative stability and fairly rapid economic growth have replaced the wild fluctuations and periodic stagnations of the early years; labour has moved from the streets into factories in

First published in Nigel Harris and John Palmer (eds), *World Crisis. Essays in Revolutionary Socialism*. London: Hutchinson & Co, 1971 the advanced countries, and industrial wages have risen far above physical subsistence in nearly all. Even the wars have changed: early capitalism's were predatory and annexationist; late capitalism's are wars of annihilation.

It would be surprising if the changes were less. Every society looks different near the end of its term in comparison with what it does near the beginning. A society as dynamic and expansionist as capitalism can be expected to be almost unrecognizably different.

Yet it remains capitalism. And socialist theory remains tied to it as it has from the start – analysing the system as it is in order to help supersede it. What follows is an analysis of the system at its latest stage.

2.

Structure

Nobody plans for capitalism as a whole. Decisions *are* taken – about the use of resources, about war and peace, about methods of production or wage rates – but they are part decisions, dispersed amongst different authorities, private and public, big and small. They are unco-ordinated but not independent: each decision influences other decisions taken elsewhere in the system, and each is influenced in its turn.

Within nation states there is now normally some co-ordination. Sometimes, as in the state-capitalist East, it is near-total at least in principle. Sometimes, as in the oligopoly-capitalist West, it is less inclusive although increasing. But internationally there is little co-ordination in practice and none in principle – independent nation states or national capitals are sovereign and the multi-national firm very nearly so. If they accommodate one another they do so out of self-interest, not because they are constrained to.

Yet a kind of order emerges from the chaos. The system

does go on from year to year and from decade to decade, through war and revolution. It does so because all capitals provide a confining environment for each; because survival within its peculiar system of interdependent autonomy promotes a more or less predictable pattern of behaviour from each.

Each needs to insure against the others' decisions, against their wilful or inexpert use of policy discretion. A firm must be able to defend its market, or match another firm's innovations. A state needs to be able to guard its capital stock from physical encroachment. In either case sheer size is the greatest insurance a single capital can normally have and growth is therefore its ultimate compulsion.

Growth can come about through conquest or takeover. It can also come about – and this is the more important historically – through accumulation, the reinvestment of savings generated within the systems. Neither is easy, the first for obvious reasons, the other because the conditions needed to induce it are so varied and complex.

Growth has to be systematically motivated. It does not simply happen. Somebody has to decide to devote freely-disposable resources as they become available to investment rather than consumption. That somebody, whether an individual or a group must be able to measure its performance against very clear criteria. It must also be very strongly motivated to make the right decisions, for primordial Adam is still not gorged, not even by affluent, late capitalism.

Neither the measurement nor the motivation has ever come easily. Today they are complicated by the very size of the capitals in play and by the related fact that the decision-takers are increasingly both salaried and anonymous. In the East a decade of debate between reformers and traditionalists and a year of open conflict (in Czechoslovakia) have still not resolved the problem. In the West, where it has never been as acute, the state or outside consultants are increasingly being invited to probe the bigger units to measure and improve their managements' performance.

A second condition for growth is that there be a continuous orderly and predictable flow of resources for expansion. Savings do not arise spontaneously, nor accumulate naturally as investment. They are also clearly not volunteered out of income by the small minority who make economic decisions – even if they were they would hardly amount to much. They must come, involuntarily as may be, from the mass of workers. But for that to happen workers must be divorced from any influence over the nature and destination of their product, which means that they must be denied positive control over the productive apparatus, which in turn means that they must be prevented in practice from holding productive property or effective rights in such property. In other words workers must be turned into proletarians and kept that way.

Two further conditions, our third and fourth, are implied in this: workers must be taxed of their main contribution to the upkeep of the system at source, in production, before they can get hold of it or realize that it is theirs – taxation of an altogether different order and kind from the relatively minor contribution to the state's upkeep they are forced to make out of received income. And that primary taxation must be systematized both in practice – so that society's institutions can be organized to police it – and in theory, so that taxation might remain unperceived as such, or at most seem as inexorable, in the nature of things, not arbitrarily imposed.

It is these last two conditions that Marx caught in his theory of value and related concepts of surplus value, exploitation and ideology or *false* consciousness. If value is the product of labour and its measure the amount of time necessarily spent working, if the ability to work is also valued on the same basis, and if equal values exchange, then the fact that workers are not in control of their product or of the productive apparatus, and are therefore bound to exchange their ability to work more or less at its value, provides both the regular hidden tax mechanism and its legitimacy. For the ability to work has less value than the product of work – the difference being surplus value, or the profits, rent and interest which sustain the system. It is a predictable surplus because based on the very slow-changing value of the ability to work. And it is an ideologically defensible surplus because, however real the inequality in bargaining power between labour and capital, the appearance of equal rights and contractual freedom is maintained – in principle at least equal values exchange and nobody is forced to work.

This last is a special case of a fifth condition for the working of a capitalist system – its overall social arrangements must be projected as permanent laws embedded in the nature of man or in the nature of economic activity or of societies or whatever, so that a single code of behaviour for the disparate unco-ordinated agencies within that society will bounce back from shared reference points which appear to be fixed and objective. The result is the typical inversions of the ruling ideology. Instead of the ability to work or labour power being seen as a saleable item, a commodity, because unco-ordinated accumulation could not take place unless it were, the ruling explanation has it that accumulation must take place in order to enlarge the job market. Instead of innovation and rationalization being seen as conditions for accumulation in a competitive setting they are presented as the ends and accumulation the means. And so on.

No society can exist without accepted modes or norms of behaviour. Most locate and elaborate them within common institutions. But in capitalism, a society without a centre, yet a society none the less, they have to be externalized or, in Marx's terms, reified and turned into fetishes. In a sense it was Marx's greatest distinction to have been able to see through the ideology to the social arrangements it distorts and to provide the socialist movement with a view of the reality from which it would need to launch its aspirations. In this lay the 'science' of his scientific socialism.

3.
The Dynamic

Marx also provided a model of how the system works and changes within these social arrangements. Reduced to the very barest essentials it is this:

Each capital is driven to raise productivity by coupling its workers with more, and more costly, machinery, while simultaneously trying to hold down wages. As this rationalization spreads, labour power becomes a smaller component of total capital (the 'organic composition of capital' rises) and smaller even in absolute terms (the 'reserve army of labour' grows); the value added in production and surplus value become smaller in relation to total investment; and so the average rate of profit falls. Booms become progressively less profitable and shorter; slumps more lasting and severe. Stagnation threatens and the system becomes increasingly restrictive. The workers' revolt against the details of repression becomes generalized into revolution; the system is overthrown and mankind emerges into freedom.

In Marx, the model assumes a closed system in which all output flows back as inputs in the form of investment goods or wage goods. There are no leaks. Yet in principle a leak could insulate the compulsion to grow from its most important consequences. If 'labour intensive' goods were to be drawn off systematically, the overall organic composition of capital would rise faster than in a closed system. If 'capital intensive' goods were drawn off the rise would be slower and, depending on the volume and composition of the leak, could even stop or be reversed. In such a case there would be no decline in the average rate of profit, no reason to expect increasingly severe slumps and so on.

Capitalism has never formed a closed system in practice. Wars and slumps have destroyed immense quantities of output, incorporating huge accumulations of value, and prevented the production of more. Capital exports have diverted and frozen other accumulations for long stretches of time. A lot has, since World War II, filtered out in the production of arms.

Each of these leaks has acted to slow the rise of the overall organic composition and the fall in the rate of profit.

4.
Imperialism

For thirty or forty years preceding World War I investment in colonial and semi-colonial territories constituted the most important leak from the system.

It was private investment and had naturally a more immediate purpose than retarding the rise in the organic compositions of capital in advanced countries. It was made specifically to finance the state, the public utilities and the productive apparatus needed to wrench backward countries into alignment with the world economy. And it did not last very long. But while it did it eased the system's capital congestion considerably and effectively.

It could not last indefinitely because investment in empire on the whole was productive investment. Individual projects might have been wasteful or misconceived. Many of them were, even in capitalist terms. The lag between the start of a project and production might have been very long. Ultimately, however, most of the investment bore fruit in greater output, larger accumulations and a renewal of the need to drain away capital. Imperialism in other words was a literally expanding system. In principle, it could postpone unhealthy capital congestion only so long as the world was not more or less colonized, and no longer.

Its end was signalled by World War I, an attempt to

share out colonial possessions more evenly. But the war itself started a train of developments that ultimately made imperialism *considered as a system of capital drain* unnecessary.[1]

In the first place wartime disruption of international trade and the real concessions that the proto-nationalist movements could exact in the circumstances led to a rash of native industrialization in the Asian colonies, the hub of the system. Not all of it could be destroyed by the imperialist powers after the war. The national movements were strengthened by it and the costs of policing empire rose commensurately.

In the imperialist countries themselves the war induced far-reaching structural change. It speeded the relative growth of manufacturing so as to dwarf all other forms of capitalist activity. It encouraged huge concentrations of capital and an even larger growth of the state as an economic agent. It thereby started a process which made planning of a sort both necessary and possible within the nation state, and so reduced the need for a colonial cushion to absorb the shock of unbalanced growth at home.

War also deepened the capital structure of the imperialist countries. The drive for self-sufficiency in food and raw materials impelled the manufacturing giants to deploy their industrial techniques in these fields, and to be sparing in the use of material inputs. In time this led to a revolutionary shift in the bias of materials (and food) production from being primarily an extractive process to being a manufacturing or near-manufacturing one. It also led to a rupture of the traditionally-imposed division of labour and trade, between the metropolitan economies and the colonies. The former became less dependent on the latter for needed raw materials just as the costs of getting them were rising.

So too with markets. As supplies from the backward countries became less important their share of world income declined, sometimes catastrophically, and so did their relative importance as customers in the world market.

But above all World War I started a process which

culminated in a permanent *unproductive* capital drain from the system, more in tune with the interests of the big technology-intensive industrial capitals that had flourished during its course.

The period in which classic imperialism stabilized the system was more or less closed by World War I. After twenty years of major adjustment and transition in which capital drain was neither systematic nor effective, World War II began a period – our own – in which the drain has once again been systematized through the permanent arms economy.

5.

The Arms Economy

The drain provided by arms budgets since World War II has constituted a far more effective mechanism for stabilizing the system than classical imperialism ever could, for it has involved a systematic destruction of values, not a relocation of their use, and it has acted in integrating the system far more effectively than any other form of expenditure.

The mechanism is essentially simple. Capital is taxed to sustain expenditure on arms and so deprived of resources that would otherwise go towards further investment. The expenditure itself constitutes a net addition to the market for 'end' goods, all the more significant for being expenditure on fast-wasting products in constant need of renewal and change. Since one obvious result of such expenditure is high employment and, as a direct consequence, rates of growth since the war amongst the highest ever, the dampening effect of such taxation is not readily apparent. But it is not absent. Were capital left to invest its entire pre-tax profit, the state creating demand as and when necessary, growth rates would have been very much higher. Finally, since arms are waste (or a 'luxury') in the strict sense that they are neither wage goods nor investment goods and therefore cannot constitute inputs into the system, they have no direct part in determining it and their production has no direct effect on profit rates overall. But since their production is a leak of high capital intensity it tends to offset the system's inbuilt bias towards declining rates of profit, as was shown in section 3.

The integrating mechanism is as simple. Arms production has a 'domino effect': starting anywhere in the system, it proliferates inexorably, compelling each major economy to enter the competitive arms race and so pulling them into a close-knit system of mutual response.

This does not imply that an arms budget was ever adopted anywhere as a means of propping up the rate of profit or of articulating the system. One can admit that governments usually step up their arms bills under protest; that the major steps have not necessarily coincided with economic downturns; that in short, *the situation* has often been seen as unfortunate, restrictive, imposed from outside or whatever; one can admit that the initial plunge into the permanent arms economy was random – without affecting the issue. The important point is that the very existence of national military machines of the current size, however happened upon, both offsets the bias towards declining profit rates and compels other national capitals to adopt a definite type of response and behaviour which requires no *policing* by some overall authority. The sum of these responses constitutes a system whose elements are both interdependent and autonomous, held together by mutual compulsion – in short a traditional capitalist system.

Once adopted, if only by chance, an arms economy becomes necessary. It is not merely that a system of mutual compulsion through military threat is more imperative than any other, but that it becomes difficult to unscramble military from economic competition. They fuse. And once that happens the contradictions of the arms economy as a system begin to crowd in.

Some of these contradictions are ideological. A military threat in today's conditions is a much more immediate and compelling argument for adopting specific policies by a national state and for policing the behaviour of independent capitals – if such exist within it – than the abstract, general principles objectified as natural laws in a more innocent age. It is an argument quickly grasped by those who need it – in Moscow or Washington, London or Pekin, Delhi or Islamabad, national defence is the supreme arbiter. Yet it is an ultimately self-defeating argument, for by sanctioning its behaviour in terms of policy-making and expediency rather than absolutes and imperatives the system is demystifying its operations, and disarming itself ideologically. Paradoxically, 'to make a profit is natural' is far stronger a rationale for the system than 'the Russians are coming'.

Other contradictions are political and economic. The arms budget's flexibility as a stabilizer *within* each national economy is set at risk by its mediation *between* economies. To expand outlay on armaments for good national economic reasons – to offset approaching recession for example – invites retaliatory escalation for equally good international strategic reasons. There is nothing to ensure that escalation stops at the point of stability. Even if the unlikely were to occur and it stopped there for one country, it would require a heroic coincidence for that to be the point of stability for others, if only because of the different sizes, structures, stages of development, sets of alliances and suchlike of the national economies grouped around a shared military technology. So that at any one time some would be favouring a reduction in armaments to safeguard their civilian competitive position, others standing pat and others pushing for further expenditure. As was shown repeatedly during the 'sixties, neither in NATO nor the Warsaw Pact, nor in the Middle East nor South and South-East Asia does there seem any way of harnessing strategic and economic expediency so that they pull in the same direction.

Nor can there be. In a *war* economy the limits to the outlay on arms are set by physical resources and the willingness of a population to endure slaughter and privation. In an *arms* economy the capacity of the economy to compete overall, in destructive potential as well as in the more traditional forms, adds a further major constraint, and with it a further nest of complications. One of these is the difficulty of gauging a 'necessary' defence effort. As it is, all but the superpowers are being squeezed out by the growing cost and complexity of the key weapons systems. Military expenditure has also taken a knock from the suicidal nature of much 'defence' equipment.

Even apart from these, the fact that *limited* preparedness – the sort implicit in an arms economy – does not necessarily draw fire, has not yet done so, makes setting the limits the subject of endless debate, particularly amongst the lesser members of the major coalitions, the ones that are least able to stand the economic pace and most attracted to the growing opportunities for trade with one another. At least one part of the stage is set for a slow competitive erosion of arms expenditure as a proportion of potential output such as took place in the West from 1953 to the present day, Cuba and Vietnam notwithstanding.

A related difficulty is the freer play for recessionary tendencies allowed by a declining ceiling on arms outlays. This can be exaggerated. Even in its classic *laissez-faire* period, the changing ratio of consumption to an economy's investible surplus put a floor to economic downswings. The higher the floor, the smaller, though the more frequent, the swings. That floor is raised at any level of arms outlay – and very much more than would appear from the normal index used (defence expenditure as a proportion of GNP) because at *any* level it is a substantial part of the investible surplus. Yet there is no denying the danger to overall stability of a decline in relative outlay.

The existence of a ceiling on outlay is important for another reason. It provides a massive incentive to increases in productivity (measured in potential deaths per dollar) and so leads to the arms industries becoming increasingly specialist and divorced from general engineering practice. Coupled with this specialization, and partly as a consequence, go a rising capital- and technology-intensity in the arms industries. Although this hardly affects their potency as a stabilizer of profits, it does reduce their value as a source of employment and social stability. It makes them less able to underpin full employment even at the same level of relative expenditure. At a declining one, and given the existence of some technological spin-off to civilian productivity, which makes the need more exacting, their ability to sustain high employment becomes increasingly questionable.

6.

The New Arms Race

For the moment, however, it is not a decline in arms expenditure that threatens the system but an enormous increase, tied to the deployment by both the US and Russia of nuclear-tipped Anti-Ballistic Missile systems and Multiple Independently targeted Re-entry Vehicles – ABMs and MIRVs.

The decision to deploy these weapons had been resisted for nearly ten years. ABMs were too complex to be expected to work, yet not complex enough in principle to cope with the tasks assigned them. They were expected to respond to surprise attack with hair-trigger sensitivity, yet provide stiff-trigger assurance against accidental or unauthorised launching. They were very prone to obsolescence from advances in offensive weapons and strategies; and three or four times as costly. Above all, they threatened to upset the Balance of Terror – each side's power to assure the other's destruction *regardless* of who strikes first.

Yet by September 1967 the US administration could no longer block them. Once missile defence came within range of technical *feasibility*, as it did in the United States by the end of the 'fifties, imputing its *deployment* to the enemy was merely a matter of time. By 1960 American military planners had endowed Russia's 'Tallin' *air*-defence system – itself designed to meet an American bomber programme that never took off – with an anti-*missile* capability it was never intended to carry. More accurate or less biased intelligence came too late to reverse the US's reactive plunge into perfecting the penetration aids that have culminated in the multi-headed missile. That plunge in its turn pushed Russia inexorably to missile defence ('Galosh', from the early 'sixties) and to a huge missile-deployment and MIRVing programme (the SS-9s, late 'sixties). As inevitably, Russia's moves precipitated the US decision on ABM and MIRV.

The logic is inescapable. At its most superficial it is fuelled by mutual distrust, by common ignorance and mutual transference of outside, 'Chinese' intentions, and by conservative 'worst-case' contingency planning. At a deeper level it reflects the pitiless inertia of a world society organized for unrestrained competition at a stage in its development when competition converges on calamity.

It is not a negotiable logic. Whatever might happen by way of formalising the ABM / MIRV round of arms escalation at the Strategic Arms Limitation Talks or anywhere else the super-powers are unlikely to reverse it. For nuclear strategy has already changed under the influence of the new, as yet undeployed, weapons, and some of the political consequences are already apparent.

Strategy has shifted from a retaliatory to a first-strike bias. Since the most effective and cheapest way to neutralize a missile defence is to overwhelm it, any ABM deployment, however feeble or rudimentary, or even any hint of such deployment, presents an irresistible argument to the other side to multiply its strike force. Since one method – arming missiles with MIRVs – is hugely productive of offensive power, and since no conceivable ABM system could neutralize it, a MIRVing programme is bound to be matched.

But MIRV parity is qualitatively different from missile parity: once the ratio of warheads per missile becomes larger than the ratio of warheads per target each side then possesses a destructive power larger than is required to overwhelm the other's missiles. Under these circumstances the attractions of a first strike, preemptive strategy in offence and of a 'launch on warning' strategy in defence become obvious. With them grows a cumulative, self-justifying pressure to raise offensive power by a truly prodigious multiple until such time as technological change will have once again reduced the ratio gap to what it was many tens of billions of dollars previously.

The cost of the new strategy is commensurate with its dangers. In its very earliest days, it was authoritatively thought that 'to maintain an effective system one would essentially have to turn over the whole system, the whole $20 billion system, every few years'.[2] Its effect has been equal to the cost. Once the 'Tet offensive' had forced the US to identify their priorities there was no doubt which way the decision would go. To the growing queue of military contractors, armed forces' strategists and Congressional lobbyists impatient for the new weapons, Vietnam quickly became a distraction from the essential American interest. Indeed, as Nixon pointed out in his tour of the region (July 1969) the whole of South-East Asia was a distraction. Even Europe – now it was Secretary of Defence, Melvin Laird, speaking – could be downgraded. And while there might be slips and sallies on the way – Nixon's surprise Spring 1970 offensive in Vietnam is one, the subsequent invasions of Laos and Cambodia are others – the direction of technology and strategy is towards Fortress America.

But that is only a beginning. The effect of the new arms race is unlikely to remain confined to military dispositions however important they may be.

7.
The Backward South

Most obviously it will have a crippling effect on the abortive capitalisms of the South.

The period now ending had at least two redeeming features for their new ruling classes. It sustained East–West competition in the supply of loans and aid, and it opened the East to trade. It therefore slowed, if only very slightly, the shrinkage of their economic space in the world.

The first of these is unlikely to last far into the 'seventies – both the nature and the size of the new weapons system run counter to it. The second might or might not last. But even if the growth of East–South trade keeps up its recent spanking pace, the cost of survival to the new, unstable and badly integrated ruling classes of the South is sure to grow even faster. For they are faced not only with rebellion and revolution within their countries, but with big power aggression and an intermittent conflict amongst themselves.

None of this would be so important were it not for the flow of increasingly deadly and costly weapons from the big powers. But the flow exists – and has been rising at 9 per cent per year in terms of volume throughout the 1950s and 1960s and much more than that in terms of firepower and destructiveness. And it is set to rise very much more in the 'seventies when the new weapons systems are phased in and conventional stocks are released.

Under these circumstances successful economic development is both an imperative for the ruling classes of the South and, for most if not all of them, literally impossible. Imperative because without it they are able neither to buy nor make the weapons that could secure their continued existence. Impossible because the developed countries are so far in advance particularly in military matters and exert such immense pressure that even after the most strenuous efforts their resources cannot hope to match their needs, while the efforts themselves could easily destroy the precarious stability on which they rest.

This paradox lies at the heart of the immense and bloody civil war raging within the South's middle class – between the section trying to keep afloat on the ebbing tide of aid, hopeful of integration in the world economy by international agreement and without violent structural change, and the section pledged to harsh autarkic development, hopeful of carving out a place in the world economy despite it; between those committed to a variant of orthodox capitalist growth and those committed to state capitalism; between the Indias and the Chinas; and within the Indias between the 'Right' and the 'Left' so-called. If the one is blind to the structural changes in the world economy underlying the South's expulsion, the other is blind to the ruinous effect these same structural changes have on the possibility of 'development in one country' be it even so large and well endowed a country as China.

Meanwhile the endless millions of peasants and workers pay for stagnation – as for the spasms of attempted development. Here and there, for a time they might appear to gain a crust, or some respite, but only as dictated by the needs of one or other protagonist in the civil war. Nowhere, despite debased talk of socialism, of democracy, of people's power, and despite an occasional independent intervention by workers do any but a section of the middle class come to power. Nor can it be otherwise. The combination of pressure and exclusion from a competitive world economy admits of no form of response, or even attempted response, other than a limitless concentration of resources in the hands of a small and ultimately oppressive local ruling class.

The world's villages can hardly destroy developed capitalism. They cannot find relief while it persists. For them, even more than for the rest of us, hope of a human existence is bound up with the prospect for revolution in the heartlands of the system.

8.

The Revolutionary Prospect

That prospect is not as far-fetched as it seemed a decade or so ago. Thirty years of boom have created a number of pressure points within developed capitalism which the new arms race might well burst open.

One of these is the growing unemployability of unskilled workers, of whom the black ghetto population in the United States is merely the most cornered, and important, group. For them the arms industry with its pronounced skill-bias is particularly inhospitable territory: in the US these industries now use proportionately 23 per cent more professional labour, 69 per cent more skilled and 25 per cent more semi-skilled labour than industry in general. Once the high technology weapons of the 'seventies displace the current generation in production, and the techniques used in their manufacture spread outwards to civilian goods, the discrepancies can only get worse.

Another pressure point is the forced drain of resources from the periphery of the system to its industrial heartlands – a reflexion of the need to create increasingly huge minimum capital concentrations in order to survive in the integrated world market of today. In almost every country of the developed world – from Quebec in Canada to Georgia in the USSR, from Scotland here to Vizcaya in Spain – this drain has revived dormant and dead nationalisms, regional and linguistic movements. Some of these movements, the struggle for civil rights in Northern Ireland for example, have become important. All are likely to grow as the giant American corporations feed on the new arms expenditure and force a countervailing gigantism on the rest of the system.

A third pressure point is the university campus, where herd logistics, primitive recruitment to ideological service and mental rough-handling have succeeded in moving several hundred thousand students the world over into sporadic confrontation with authority and a significant, if small, minority into political opposition. As the frightening irrationality of the new arms race unfolds it will become increasingly difficult to prevent the student mass from reacting permanently.

These are weak points in the system, but not the weakest. So long as they form no part of its major, seismic, fault – the conflict between labour and capital in production – they can do little more than serve as foci for revolutionary thought and organization, not of revolutionary action.

However, the arms economy has not passed over the broader class struggle. Under its benign influence the size of the dominant capitals has grown so enormous and the space between them become so decompressed that survival as an independent capital has become dependent in many cases on wrenching entire national economies into new shapes and on making entire national working classes bear its strains, whether in the form of wage freezes or forced labour mobility or unemployment or whatever. At the same time the long boom has diluted the workers' positive commitment to the system and eroded the institutional forms – the mass social-democratic and Communist Parties in particular – in which it used to be expressed, so that now their tolerance of strain is far less than that of their fathers. The result is that economic growth and stability have not only become a familiar condition within developed capitalism but a necessary one for its proper functioning just at a time when continued growth requires instability in the form of structural adaptation and change.

The rise and fall of Gaullist France is a spectacular illustration. De Gaulle was brought in, in 1958, to preside over the liquidation of an old-time imperialist war in Algeria, over the reconstitution of French industry into a large-unit, technically advanced structure to cope with the Common Market, and over a military transformation that would turn a conscripted para-police force into a professional modern army. He held down labour costs so successfully that by 1966 French industrial wages were second lowest in the Common Market and hours worked the longest. Without draconian measures unthinkable in peacetime it was impossible to keep them that way for long and indeed in May–June 1968 the regime was rocked by the biggest general strike in history – bigger by far than the British General Strike, of 1926 bigger even than the strike accompanying the Russian Revolution – and one with strong insurrectionary impulses.

In the event the workers were bought off. The 'more' they had asked for and been refused was granted as soon as they began to question the accepted rules for allocating it, as soon that is as they reached for control. French capital, with US and German help, found the resources to buy them off. But French capital has been hammered in the process. It is unlikely again to try to assert its independence as a key centre of decision-taking on a world scale.

It was not only French capital that was caught in the strobe lights of May–June 1968 but the system as such. Nothing was in play in Paris that is not to be found in some degree everywhere else. On the contrary, if de Gaulle's paradox was the need to dispense wage restraint, enforced mobility of labour, legislative controls and deflation on an already highly employed and ideologically detached working class, then most of the major centres of national capital are edging towards a gaullist paradox of their own. Scale for scale the costs and results of maintaining competitiveness in an increasingly compressed and unstable economic environment were no greater for French capitalism than they are for German or British or European capitalism; and scale for scale they are also no greater for these than are the cost and results for the US or Russia of maintaining military effectiveness within the terms of the new arms race. We have seen that the costs are likely to be prodigious. The results could be even more so. For capitalism in its latest phase is again creating the conditions for a convergence of working-class protest and revolutionary politics that could change the world.

Whether or not that convergence takes place in the 'seventies depends as much on revolutionaries as on anything discussed in this chapter. But that is to trespass on areas covered elsewhere in this volume.

1. As a political system, as an ideology and as a system of attitudes, Imperialism continued long after its base narrowed. But this is not the place for a full analysis.

2. Dr John S. Foster, Director, Defense Research and Engineering, in US Senate, *US Armament and Disarmament Problems*. Hearings before the Sub-committee on Disarmament of the Committee on Foreign Relations, 3 February to 3 March 1969, p15.

Part One

THE CENTRE

2. Waste: US 1970

I.

Productive and Unproductive Activity in Capitalism

There has never been serious disagreement with the central proposition of political economy – that capitalism depends for survival on the growth of its productive apparatus. The early political economists took it as read. Marx made it the centre-piece of his analysis. But there has also never been any real agreement about the sources of that growth. For good reason. Like any other class society, capitalism transfers surplus from productive workers to the rulers. Unlike any other class society, capitalism projects that transfer on its ideological screen as an exchange of equivalents. Except by fortunate chance or as a result of criminal activity, no one on that screen gets anything for nothing. If the capitalist or members of his supporting cast receive income, it is because they are engaged in productive activity; if housewives don't, it must be because their labour, however necessary it might be, is unproductive.

In other words, as a system of competition capitalism depends on the growth of capital; as a class system it depends on obscuring the sources of that growth. And since it needs to act on what it dare not perceive, its custodians—military planners and executive government – have been forced to develop rules of thumb about worth and waste[1] while the conceptualizers and ideologists, led by the economists, puzzle with words.[2]

Like the custodians, revolutionaries need to know what is essential to capitalism; unlike them they need have no conceptual inhibitions and no truck with the ideologists. We, better than anyone, ought to be able to define what is productive in terms of the system's purposes, if not in the terms it uses to describe them.[3]

Productive labour and necessary labour

If the fundamental drive in capitalism is growth of capital, only workers employed directly by capital *to make more* capital can be productive;[4] the others are not, although they might be necessary for society and even essential for capital itself. In the peculiar logic of the system a gentleman farmer is productive but a market gardener working on his own is not; a window cleaner is not productive, but one supplied by a window-cleaning contractor is.

In the early days of capitalism, this peculiar logic differentiated very clearly between two groups of *indirect* workers: those, like engineers, mechanics or managers who 'contribute in one way or another to the production of the commodity' and who were considered productive because they were normally on capital's payroll; and those, like teachers, doctors, mothers who produce or contribute to the production of *the* commodity – labour-power – but who were considered unproductive[5] because they were not usually employed. They worked on their own account.[6] One group was clearly no less necessary to capitalism than the other. The distinction between them lay rather in the degree to which their services were shared between the system and the larger non-capitalist society in which it was embedded.

When capital's criteria for productiveness were being

formulated, the brute labour-power it needed was being driven and drawn for the most part from outside the system; its producers, in so far as they were engaged in producing labour-power were doing so incidentally, as part of activities that were characteristic of the non-capitalist societies of the time. It was easy then for capital to avoid employing them, and paying them; as easy for capital to shunt the cost of producing its labour-power on to the declining societies it was undermining in any case, as it was difficult for it to avoid investing in the indirect labour-power that was unique to its own mode of production.

Times changed and so did the balance between the system and society. Capitalism became too large and complex to rely on virtually free supplies from outside. Capital had to provide for its own necessities, and so to take on the responsibility for reproducing the society which provided them. The individual capital, the system's basic unit, grew with the task to embrace the state and the entire national capital more or less. The original distinction between necessary and productive labour was undermined; and with it the distinction between indirect labour engaged in producing labour-power and indirect labour producing all other commodities.

Employment by capital and expansion of capital

If the ageing of capitalism or, more specifically, the enormous growth in the size and responsibilities of its component units, brought into direct relation with capital many socially-necessary activities that were for good reason considered unproductive for the system in Marx's day, it also opened a gulf between the two criteria of productiveness that he used interchangeably – employment by capital and augmenting capital.

Marx was not blind to the distinction but he did not need to elaborate on it. In the reality he was considering – early nineteenth century Britain in which the industrial bourgeoisie was freeing itself from anachronistic practices, and political economy was freeing it from anachronistic categories – the two criteria were consonant with one another. Capital employed only such labour-power as would lead to its 'self-expansion'. And all the rest, the 'incidental expenses of production' including the expense of maintaining state and church, and the cost of the indirect labour spent in the production of labour-power, could be lumped together in one portmanteau category – payment for unproductive labour. He foresaw clearly enough the costly consequences to the capitalist class of its assuming state power and the social and ideological responsibilities that go with it,[7] but that was for the future. It was not allowed to affect the analysis.

But now that capital is king, and has pressed vast sections of world society into its service, the two criteria are no longer congruous. Millions of workers employed directly by capital produce goods and services which it cannot use for further expansion under any conceivable circumstances. They are productive by one criterion and unproductive by the other.

Clearly a choice has to be made of the essential, rather than the institutional criterion. The choice should make it possible to distinguish between the rising cost of maintaining the social framework of the system out of its own resources and the declining costs of production within it and so highlight the ageing of the system. Given the need to choose, productive labour today must be defined as labour whose final output is or can be an input into further production. Only such labour can work for capital's self-expansion. In the final analysis, all output able to sustain the ability to work, that is all output used by or consumed directly or indirectly by productive labour, is the product of productive labour; all other output is produced by unproductive labour.

This definition makes no distinction between employing agencies, and so avoids the anachronism of excluding state expenditure as unproductive per se[8] or non-productive.[9] It also avoids the utopian trap of judging productiveness by criteria that might be suitable for a future socialist society or 'in the light of objective reason'.[10]

Within a logic which is the system's own, it focusses on the decay of capital as much as it does on its growth, on the system's inability to use its output as much as on its ability to produce it. For that reason the definition is right for now, the period of the permanent arms economy, the final stage in the system's existence, in which the further expansion of capital is limited by the particular forms it is compelled to adopt.

The distinction between productive and unproductive labour within capitalism extends by analogy to the instruments of labour and to the surplus itself. Plant and equipment that can be used only by unproductive labour or that are normally so used are clearly waste. Surplus embodied in such waste apparatus or expended in unproductive employment is wasted, not accumulated. In other words the labour, materials and equipment devoted to sustaining unproductive labour and maintaining a waste sector is waste. And the physical output in which this activity is embodied is sterile. It cannot be used productively. To spell it out, in late capitalism only part of surplus can be used for the expansion of capital. The rest is waste product.

Waste product and productive surplus

Marx did not draw these structural conclusions from his distinction between productive and unproductive labour. Nor did most of his critics and followers. Although he assumed, realistically, that capitalists consume unproductively as well as productively, that is, some part of their consumption out of surplus – personal consumption – does not go into maintaining either the ability to work or the apparatus of production, and although at the extreme, in his model of Simple Reproduction, he assumed that *all* capitalist consumption is unproductive, he yet considered productive the labour spent on that unproductive consumption, labour – to repeat – that does not lead to capital growth. In terms of one of his criteria of productiveness it certainly is. It is labour employed by capital. It is productive also in terms of the common-sense view that labour spent on keeping some people in idleness must produce a *surplus*, particularly when that surplus looks physically very much like necessities and its technique of production is nearly the same,[11] when, that is, waste-goods are not immediately recognisable as such.

But in terms of Marx's second, and essential, criterion – the production of surplus *used or useable for the expansion of capital* – labour spent on maintaining unproductive consumption, *labour spent on waste-goods production*, including labour spent on the technical apparatus necessary for waste goods production, is unproductive. It is surplus transforming and surplus absorbing labour – not surplus-creating.

Classing waste-goods production as unproductive rather than productive activity has far-reaching consequences: if it is productive, there can be no inner barriers to the growth of the system. True, waste grows and that's a dreadful waste, but so does waste production, and that's productive. You can discount the waste or count, with the economists, its contribution to net national income. Depending on the way you're looking at it, the system grows or doesn't. The choice is arbitrary.

If waste-goods production is productive there can also be no final constraints on the adaptability of the system. All that would be needed to change its nature is to change end-uses, to do something about final demand. For, in this keynesianized marxism represented by the *Monthly Review* school, intermediates in production have function but no substance.

More fundamentally, classing waste-goods production as productive makes nonsense of the concept of necessary labour – the labour required to maintain the ability to work, or more loosely, the labour including the indirect labour required to produce the normal constituents of a worker's standard of living. It makes nonsense of the concept of surplus as all output – at ruling cost – over and above necessary output, and therefore makes nonsense of the labour theory of value and everything that flows from it (including the locating of the basic conflict in the system at the point of surplus-production).

Capitalism now employs hundreds of millions of people who by no stretch of the imagination can be said to contribute to its growth. From its inverted point of view, if not explicitly in its terms, they are unproductive even if they are necessary to maintain class rule and the independence of individual capitals. Their consumption is unproductive. The equipment they work with is waste. The surplus goods they create and absorb are sterile. Together these constitute a huge waste sector within an increasingly maleficent system.

2.
Surplus Goods Production: The Waste Sector

There is no way of measuring the waste sector directly. The data do not exist. But we can get a view of its size if we define it as:

production generated directly and indirectly by military expenditure; plus

production generated directly and indirectly by unproductive government expenditure other than military; plus

production generated in waste industries and the waste sectors of productive industries, and production generated directly and indirectly by them, including production generated by gross fixed investment in these industries and sectors; plus

production generated directly or indirectly by the personal consumption expenditure of workers employed directly or indirectly in waste production; of employees in 'unproductive occupations'; and personal consumption expenditure out of business and property income; less multiple counting.

Production generated by military expenditure:
This is the prime expense incurred by the system for maintaining independent capitals. The overwhelming bulk of expenditure goes on goods and services that cannot, in any circumstances, be reclaimed for further production; and the little that can – outlays on occupational training, or on publicly-used transport facilities for example – is more than offset by expenditure ostensibly productive and actually undertaken for military ends on a 'freelance' or speculative basis.

Production generated by unproductive government
expenditure other than military:
Most central or, in the US, Federal government outlay and some local government outlay is devoted to maintaining class division and the individual's place within a class, not to expanding production. Some of the outlay is spent on coercion (police, prisons, law); some on material persuasion (state pensions, veterans' allowances, farm subsidies, business administration); and some on both (general administration).
The following categories of US Federal Government outlay are considered waste:
Space research and technology
General government (general administration; general property and records management; central personnel management and employment; net interest paid; other)
Old age and retirement benefits
Civilian safety (police; correction)
Veterans' benefits and services (disability and pension allowances; insurance; administration and other services)

Regulation of commerce and finance
Stabilization of farm prices and income

These accounted for 60·6 per cent of federal government non-military expenditure in 1970. Using the same categories 18·1 per cent of state and local government expenditure were taken as waste-generating in that year.

*Production generated in and by waste-industries
and the waste sectors of the partially-waste industries;
including production generated by
gross fixed investment in these industries
and sectors:*

Waste industries are those whose outputs are in principle unassimilable as inputs into further production, either because they are a surrogate for personal expenditure by capitalists (such as business entertainment) or because they are an expense of surplus-distribution amongst sections of the ruling class (such as finance). Where they include a productive sector, as they occasionally do, it has been abstracted.

The following industries are treated as waste:
Finance and insurance
Real estate and rental (excluding maintenance and repair construction)
Business services
Business travel, entertainment and gifts

Partially-waste industries are those whose outputs are in principle assimilable as inputs into further production although in practice a proportion is systematically drained off into unproductive use. The partially-waste industries form a huge category. In almost every industry the production process is invaded by the sales effort – to the extent of a tenth of consumer expenditure in the US, in one estimate.[12] Large parts of industrial activity are devoted to financial (as distinct from material) record keeping.

There is waste associated with planned obsolescence; the building and maintenance of prestige offices in central business districts; and so on.

Most of this cannot be quantified easily or at all, and we have been forced to select the most obvious of the major industries in this category (at the cost of severely understating our case).

These are:

New construction
Trade
Office, computing and accounting machines
Motor vehicles and equipment
Automobile repair and services
Office supplies

The degree to which these are wasteful and waste-inducing as well as the derivation of the results are given later in Section 3 of this essay.

Production generated by personal consumption expenditure
of workers employed directly or indirectly
in waste production, of employees in 'unproductive occupations';
and personal consumption expenditure
out of business and property income:

'Waste occupations' fulfil the coercive, supervisory, espionage and persuading functions normally associated with government, but required *within* the productive sector to maintain class rule. They also fulfil functions in selling. Using US job classifications as a rough guide, these 'waste occupations' are:

Accountants and auditors
Clergymen
Sales engineers
Funeral directors and embalmers
Personnel and labour relations men
Public relations men and publicity
Religious workers

Social and welfare workers
Social scientists
Farm managers
Managers, officials and proprietors (except self-employed)
Agents (not elsewhere classified – nec)
Bank tellers
Bookkeepers
Collectors, bill and account
Decorators and window dressers
Foremen (nec)
Furriers
Taxicab drivers and chauffeurs
Private household workers
Attendants, professional and personal service (nec)
Elevator operators (except hospital)
Guards, watchmen and doorkeepers
Marshals and constables
Policemen and detectives
Sheriffs and bailiffs
Watchmen (crossing) and bridge tenders
Farm foremen
Lawyers and judges
Insurance adjusters, examiners, and investigators
Sales workers (except salesmen and sales clerks in non-waste trade)
The same proportion of the category 'occupation not reported' as
the ratio of those in waste occupations to total employ-
ment.

There is one segment of waste personal consumption
which we have ignored although it is important – personal consumption out of salaries containing surplus, that is personal consumption out of high executive and professional incomes which
are classed as 'earned' for tax and ideological reasons, but which
are actually larger than anything that could be justified in terms
of output.

A preliminary exercise shows that this category of personal expenditure would add something like 2·2 per cent of gross output, and of final demand, to the waste sector, but the method we adopted was so crude we prefer to understate our results than assert too much too baldly.

3.
Methods and Sources

The method is based on a static input-output model. Final demand vectors for the various types of waste were estimated, the waste industries and waste sectors of the partially waste industries being treated as exogenous. These vectors were then multiplied by the corresponding total requirements matrix to find the induced output generated by each category of waste. Subtracting from gross output by industry gives productive output by industry. The waste industries were regarded as having no productive output, and the outputs of the partially-waste industries were reduced first by the amount of waste they themselves produced, then further by the output generated by the other forms of waste in their productive sectors. The waste final demand vectors were subtracted from total final demand to give productive final demand. All calculations are in 1958 us dollars, implicit price deflators being used where necessary.

The Input-output Matrix
An 82 × 82 matrix for the us in 1970 was given by the Bureau of Labor Statistics, us Department of Commerce, as were gross output levels by industry. The waste industries were deleted from the transaction form of this matrix, and the partially-waste industries reduced in the requisite proportions. New direct and total requirements matrices were obtained, corresponding to the smaller transactions matrix.

The Waste Vectors

1. *Military expenditure*

Military expenditure for 1970, distributed by industry, was published in 'Employment Effects of Reduced Defense Spending', by R.P.Oliver.[13] The industrial classification used is the same as that in the BLS matrix, except that 'Communications, except Radio and TV' and 'Radio and TV' are combined as one industry. The figure was split in two in the proportions of these industries' gross outputs.

2. *Federal Government Non-military Expenditure*

The waste categories defined in Section 2 of this essay amounted to 60·6 per cent of federal non-military expenditure[14]. Figures for federal military and non-military expenditure in 1970 and 1963 were given by Stephen P. Dresch in the preliminary draft of a report for the Department of Economic and Social Affairs of the United Nations.[15] The 82 sectors used by the BLS are here consolidated into 35 industries. Total federal expenditure in 1963, in 82 industries, was published in the 1963 Input-Output Tables of the US.[16] Federal military expenditure in 1963, from Dresch in 35 industries, was disaggregated using Oliver's 1970 figures. Subtraction from the published total federal final demand vector gave a 1963 federal non-military vector in 82 industries. Dresch's 1970 non-military vector was disaggregated to 82 industries using this vector. Briefly, at the 35 industry level, the federal non-military final demand vector is that supplied by Dresch, but to disaggregate it, 1963 figures were used. The resultant vector was multiplied by a factor of 0·606 to give federal government non-military waste final demand.

3. State and Local Government Waste Expenditure

State and local government expenditure were treated in the same way as federal expenditures, Dresch's 1970 figures being broken down using 1963 figures. The waste factor in this case was 0·181.[17]

4. The Waste Industries

The inputs of the waste industries (except those from each other) were added, industry by industry, to form the waste industry final demand vector. Maintenance and repair construction in the real estate and rental industry was counted as productive and excluded.

5. The Partially-Waste Industries

As will easily be seen, we have derived the waste proportions in our six partially-waste industries very crudely, but in each case the degree of waste has been greatly understated.

Trade

In so far as trade distributes necessary consumption goods and the equipment necessary directly and indirectly for their production it is productive; otherwise it is waste. To isolate the necessary distributive function, we compared employment in trade in two large, equally class-ridden economies with comparable-sized working populations, but with a markedly different organization of distribution – the US and the USSR. Using, as a rough measure of the necessary minimum proportionate size of a distributive network, the ratio of employment in trade to total population in Russia in 1964 (the latest year for which figures were readily available) US trade could be deflated to some 22 per cent of its actual size – 78 per cent of activity in trade is waste.[18]

Office, Computing and Accounting Machines, and Office Supplies

The proportion of clerical and kindred workers in waste occupations was found to be 18·93 per cent. This was the figure used for the waste sectors of these two industries.

Motor Vehicles and Equipment, and Auto Repair and Services

Company cars were considered a form of waste, being essentially a tax evasion mechanism, rather than the provision of necessary transport. Since non-household purchases of new passenger cars amounted to 15·95 per cent of all such purchases in 1970, this was the proportion treated as waste.[19] This is an overestimate in that passenger cars do not form the entire output of the industry, but since there are so many other, far larger, waste mechanisms permeating this industry,[20] which are difficult to evaluate, it was allowed to stand. The auto repair industry was reduced in the same proportion as the motor vehicle industry.

New Construction

There is a breakdown of the value of new construction into the categories: housing, industrial buildings, office buildings, service stations and repair garages, and stores and other mercantile buildings.[21] This gives a 13,000 place sample of private construction, but since the 13,000 place universe accounts for approximately 85 per cent of all new residential construction in the United States, it was taken as representative of the industry as a whole. 18·93 per cent of office buildings were taken as being wasteful, the proportion of waste office workers.

78·04 per cent of stores and mercantile buildings were reckoned waste, the proportion of waste trade. 15·95 per cent of service stations and garages were taken as waste, the proportion of waste in the auto repair industry. The combination of these figures gives a level of waste of 6·96 per cent in the new construction industry.

The partially-waste industries final demand vector was formed by the addition of these proportions of their inputs (except those from the waste industries which have been deleted from the model).

6. Gross Fixed Investment in the Waste Industries and the Waste Sectors of the Partially-Waste Industries

The figures for this vector are from Dresch *et al.*

7. Waste Personal Consumption Expenditures

First, the number of people involved was estimated, then their earnings, and then their personal consumption expenditures.

For the purposes of this calculation, the economy was divided into 16 major industries. Using detailed statistics of occupation by industry for the 1960 civilian labour force,[22] the number of people in waste occupations was found. Assuming, for want of more recent figures, that the occupation structure of industries remained unchanged, the numbers in waste occupations in 1970 were obtained.

To these figures were added military generated civilian employment and military employment.[23] To remove the double counting of waste occupations within military generated production, it was assumed that the density of these waste occupations is the same in military and non-military generated production within any industry.

The employment in the waste industries, and the proportion of the employment in the partially waste industries were then added. Again, to avoid double counting, the density of waste occupations and military generated employment was assumed constant throughout the partially-waste industries.

This last set of figures gives the number of people in waste employment because of their occupation, their employing industry, or the end-use of their product.

The figure for each industry was then multiplied by the average wage or salary earnings for that industry,[24] and these induced earnings were then summed.

The proportion of these earnings spent on personal consumption was taken to be the ratio of personal consumption expenditures to personal income for 1970.[25]

The waste personal consumption sum was distributed according to the personal consumption expenditure vector for 1969.[26]

8. *Personal Consumption Expenditure from Business and Property Income*

The percentage of business and property income spent on personal consumption in 1960–61 was estimated in the following way. The proportion of business and property income received by a given income bracket[27] was multiplied by the ratio of personal consumption expenditure to total income for that bracket[28] and the results summed over all income brackets. This assumes an unchanged income distribution between 1960–61 and 1962, and that consumption expenditure comes from earned and unearned income in equal proportions.

This percentage was then applied to business and property income received in 1970.[29]

The resulting personal consumption expenditure figure was distributed by industry according to the 1969 personal consumption expenditure vector, and was then adjusted for the fact that a large proportion of this income is received by the upper income brackets whose expenditure patterns differ significantly from the norm. Using percentage breakdowns of consumption expenditure by type (food, clothing, housing, etc.) and income bracket,[30] the industries of the vector were fitted to these expenditure types, and the elements of the vector weighted by the ratio of expenditure by income bracket to average expenditure for 1960–61, in the proportions of business and property income received by income brackets.

Although no more than an approximation to the 1970 expenditure patterns of this income bracket, this was felt to be at least some improvement on the original vector.

To avoid double-counting the waste generated in the waste sectors of the partially-waste industries, the inputs from

Table 1: Waste Output of Industry Distributed by Waste Category: US 1970

Industry	Military military	Federal government non-military	State and local government	Waste industry outputs	Waste industry inputs	Investment in waste industry	Waste personal consumption	Consumption from business and property income	Total waste	Waste as percentage gross output
1 Livestock and Livestock products	2425·44	-10·20	43·70	0·00	3243·97	16·62	7893·18	4706·72	18319·43	57·86
2 Other agricultural products	1721·79	-37·98	-19·30	0·00	3444·43	52·64	561·54	3385·66	14162·72	51·79
3 Forestry and fishery products	127·24	-61·91	32·50	0·00	217·77	48·63	359·99	247·69	972·15	51·27
4 Agricultural, forestry and fishery services	124·77	4·60	32·41	0·00	408·72	5·83	378·94	228·12	1183·38	61·25
5 Iron and ferroalloy ores mining	178·05	16·56	32·90	0·00	269·48	52·69	188·64	141·52	879·85	40·29
6 Nonferrous metal ores mining	207·70	18·36	23·92	0·00	205·58	32·38	144·56	109·21	741·71	47·98
7 Coal mining	250·26	27·26	46·51	0·00	548·77	33·18	461·45	206·11	1573·54	45·29
8 Crude petroleum and natural gas	1657·60	51·00	229·84	0·00	2440·33	109·36	3058·93	1832·23	9379·29	57·15
9 Stone and clay mining and quarrying	86·58	21·87	48·90	0·00	334·04	99·84	13·24	93·87	808·34	31·16
10 Chemical and fertilizer mineral mining	63·51	5·21	26·50	0·00	98·46	7·28	101·54	74·73	377·23	23·03
11 New construction	543·54	1008·18	3072·00	5169·40	1046·16	5382·00	0·00	0·00	15175·12	20·43
12 Maintenance and repair construction	1197·41	131·16	821·12	0·00	10416·16	54·88	1476·71	845·38	14942·81	78·25
13 Ordnance and accessories	5538·50	178·63	2·64	0·00	10·30	0·59	107·02	173·02	6010·71	66·57
14 Food and kindred products	6976·21	-6·75	182·57	0·00	5154·98	26·15	23384·76	1409·43	49927·36	56·85
15 Tobacco manufactures	48·41	0·01	0·25	0·00	250·20	0·07	1976·69	836·42	3546·04	52·82
16 Broad and narrow fabrics, yarn and thread mills	1604·05	78·25	61·53	0·00	771·49	38·36	4791·63	4056·80	11402·10	70·22
17 Miscellaneous textile goods and floor coverings	412·90	3·84	22·06	0·00	497·69	26·15	1158·01	909·67	3030·32	51·25
18 Apparel	1879·83	72·27	48·52	0·00	2281·87	6·68	6708·21	6064·83	15002·21	60·38
19 Miscellaneous fabricated textile products	335·91	-124·27	11·19	0·00	348·91	15·63	1032·96	781·27	2401·59	60·28
20 Lumber and wood products, except containers	516·11	113·31	358·10	0·00	1816·55	527·15	855·48	648·47	4835·18	42·70
21 Wooden containers	36·42	-6·93	2·43	0·00	117·25	3·84	66·52	43·84	263·37	49·23
22 Household furniture	418·36	11·76	27·92	0·00	747·71	26·58	1201·07	938·41	2698·81	53·93
23 Other furniture and fixtures	68·55	27·50	123·46	0·00	71·14	22·58	99·47	80·02	492·73	16·33
24 Paper and allied products, except containers	1090·51	12·74	192·57	0·00	5744·46	127·94	2427·88	1882·93	11579·04	61·32
25 Paperboard containers and boxes	495·73	5·81	51·55	0·00	1190·06	40·69	1089·10	744·88	3617·82	52·93
26 Printing and Publishing	840·97	66·41	232·74	0·00	13060·78	24·68	2028·21	1422·07	17675·86	85·55
27 Chemicals and selected chemical products	2095·72	175·94	310·60	0·00	2902·57	194·91	3163·02	2308·84	11151·60	41·67
28 Plastics and synthetic materials	914·16	52·91	85·81	0·00	2037·57	84·61	1744·27	1443·52	5447·77	45·49
29 Drugs, cleaning and toilet preparations	1006·53	10·41	179·17	0·00	672·18	19·67	3286·86	1950·47	7125·28	49·14
30 Paints and allied products	181·09	8·95	58·97	0·00	637·88	43·06	264·34	198·86	1393·16	50·28
31 Petroleum refining and related industries	3062·82	85·69	410·90	0·00	3691·81	197·13	5363·29	3558·73	16370·37	55·60
32 Rubber and miscellaneous plastics products	1394·31	66·16	149·49	0·00	2333·28	159·50	2394·79	2093·03	8590·57	50·36
33 Leather tanning and industrial leather products	85·77	1·32	2·55	0·00	43·44	1·59	268·63	239·62	642·93	70·50
34 Footwear and other leather products	333·91	1·37	2·71	0·00	97·66	1·13	1104·98	997·49	2539·25	74·44
35 Glass and glass products	315·34	16·25	56·13	0·00	563·64	42·06	627·04	406·69	2027·17	51·40
36 Stone and clay products	474·96	119·95	348·36	0·00	1539·78	526·32	522·89	419·22	3951·49	30·47
37 Primary iron and steel manufacturing	232·38	241·87	452·73	0·00	3556·67	752·86	2511·76	1889·18	11797·45	36·01
38 Primary nonferrous metal manufacturing	2248·18	164·08	246·89	0·00	2017·13	343·83	1421·33	1086·65	7528·00	70·50
39 Metal containers	238·48	3·57	15·48	0·00	223·68	6·30	676·14	409·48	1573·14	48·48
40 Heating, plumbing and structural metal products	393·87	132·48	346·74	0·00	1325·39	525·03	262·52	237·12	3223·75	23·56
41 Stampings, screw machine products and bolts	665·86	27·68	62·87	0·00	729·60	96·23	732·01	523·89	2838·13	43·24

	1	2	3	4	5	6	7	8	9	Total	%
42 Other fabricated metal products	917·26	67·88	149·93	0·00	0·00	1400·71	230·57	1276·25	912·46	4955·07	40·51
43 Engines and turbines	337·96	42·57	9·75	0·00	0·00	332·90	14·30	196·61	180·80	1148·89	27·94
44 Farm machinery and equipment	57·01	7·43	16·18	0·00	0·00	377·57	6·57	83·78	65·31	613·85	18·60
45 Construction, mining and oil field machinery	211·73	33·88	51·77	0·00	0·00	235·53	34·42	84·94	62·85	715·12	14·58
46 Materials handling machinery and equipment	150·54	32·30	21·02	0·00	0·00	97·48	33·03	28·93	27·40	390·71	16·16
47 Metalworking machinery and equipment	533·04	22·38	44·35	0·00	0·00	484·16	50·36	293·02	236·31	1663·62	23·99
48 Special industry machinery and equipment	101·92	7·77	16·30	0·00	0·00	194·48	11·37	122·69	105·54	560·08	11·28
49 General industrial machinery and equipment	522·77	32·41	60·94	0·00	0·00	458·59	78·35	257·07	208·36	1618·49	21·82
50 Machine shop products	861·40	41·27	55·95	1939·19	0·00	353·34	33·99	202·20	158·81	1706·96	46·02
51 Office, computing and accounting machines	290·32	30·78	17·22	0·00	0·00	1101·66	300·01	59·67	43·03	3781·88	36·92
52 Service industry machines	234·28	25·57	86·30	0·00	0·00	428·60	38·09	356·55	270·98	1440·37	24·52
53 Electric industrial equipment and apparatus	1043·24	71·90	78·63	0·00	0·00	534·03	91·55	431·05	361·69	2612·08	26·09
54 Household appliances	481·46	11·92	32·34	0·00	0·00	155·84	35·95	1643·98	1271·08	3632·57	50·22
55 Electric lighting and wiring equipment	359·83	28·07	75·44	0·00	0·00	400·24	106·71	398·71	305·10	1674·10	41·92
56 Radio, TV and communication equipment and supply	6261·38	208·63	43·42	0·00	0·00	958·66	44·26	1823·99	1547·78	10888·11	51·03
57 Electronic components and accessories	2156·21	72·02	21·69	0·00	0·00	429·15	39·78	775·32	635·26	4121·85	37·25
58 Miscellaneous electrical machinery and equipment	285·76	13·63	15·58	0·00	0·00	43·28	30·78	406·55	320·52	1520·10	47·09
59 Motor vehicles equipment	300·44	123·51	319·51	0·00	8923·55	4017·36	2066·95	8583·07	5403·15	32440·14	57·98
60 Aircraft and parts	832·17	-25·47	6·02	0·00	0·00	152·70	6·75	98·05	115·33	8676·16	43·87
61 Other transportation equipment	1534·29	287·93	26·63	0·00	0·00	241·85	14·83	1193·83	1844·94	5144·31	56·64
62 Scientific and controlling instruments	984·10	19·29	75·68	0·00	0·00	604·90	53·36	688·08	445·00	2652·79	34·43
63 Optical, ophthalmic and photographic equipment	544·90	81·07	25·98	0·00	0·00	1325·82	2·41	589·04	423·79	2272·09	44·02
64 Miscellaneous manufacturing	679·13	18·33	157·63	0·00	0·00	940·42	25·05	2195·60	1658·82	6060·38	63·28
65 Transportation and warehousing	5773·76	104·59	585·24	0·00	0·00	5015·29	432·97	8305·21	9940·22	34542·41	61·10
66 Communications; except radio and tv broadcasting	1418·21	55·46	159·70	0·00	0·00	3167·32	62·89	3508·99	1331·59	11552·13	51·30
67 Radio and TV broadcasting	50·14	0·00	5·70	0·00	0·00	765·93	0·00	0·00	0·00	3223·15	85·74
68 Electric, gas, water and sanitary services	2935·35	148·51	524·01	0·00	0·00	2204·44	233·67	7888·51	1755·50	21161·48	49·78
69 Wholesale and retail trade	2497·14	54·45	134·55	124710·26	0·00	2204·44	6901·97	8033·45	6053·06	150589·30	94·23
70 Finance and Insurance	0·00	0·00	0·00	39325·00	0·00	0·00	0·00	0·00	0·00	39325·00	100·00
71 Real estate and rental	0·00	0·00	0·00	104951·00	0·00	0·00	0·00	0·00	0·00	104951·00	100·00
72 Hotels; Personal and repair services exc. auto	1483·68	25·39	62·07	0·00	0·00	2332·59	10·90	4524·48	2848·88	11277·99	67·32
73 Business services	0·00	0·00	0·00	50364·00	0·00	0·00	0·00	0·00	0·00	50364·00	100·00
74 Research and development	472·37	1·83	2·51	0·00	0·00	31·81	3·08	51·86	29·13	592·59	94·21
75 Automobile repair and services	647·58	16·58	88·26	1999·33	0·00	2237·16	62·16	2081·85	1392·09	8525·28	68·10
76 Amusements	530·53	3·61	-26·44	0·00	0·00	1324·67	2·42	1578·99	637·86	4051·65	60·59
77 Medical, educational services and nonprofit organizations	3296·68	136·78	118·26	0·00	0·00	603·96	15·16	11297·20	3615·71	19103·75	49·51
78 Federal government enterprises	334·44	48·71	157·15	0·00	0·00	3353·52	25·14	790·17	414·17	5123·31	65·02
79 State and local government enterprises	652·07	175·97	95·98	0·00	0·00	2520·40	47·97	1735·72	752·25	5980·36	72·88
80 Gross imports of goods and services	4806·61	273·83	237·35	0·00	0·00	3541·33	259·01	5429·89	6064·55	20612·56	41·35
81 Business travel, entertainment and gifts	0·00	0·00	0·00	9187·00	0·00	0·00	0·00	0·00	0·00	9187·00	100·00
82 Office supplies	116·46	32·44	159·32	513·00	0·00	1023·13	8·70	135·55	77·36	2065·97	76·23
Sum	99970·77	5148·72	12149·83	34708·73		131948·46	21196·79	168424·46	113762·77	146463800	61·43
% Total Output	6·83	0·35	0·83	23·70		9·01	1·45	11·50	7·77		61·43
% Total Waste	11·11	0·57	1·35	38·58		14·67	2·36	18·72	12·64		100·00

each of these industries to the final demand vectors were reduced by the waste factors of the industry.

That proportion of the waste supported personal consumption vector due to military generated employment was shifted to the military vector, which therefore included both Department of Defense expenditures and the induced personal consumption expenditures.

The resulting final demand vectors were each multiplied by the total requirements matrix to find the induced output levels in the rest of the economy.

Table 1 shows the proportion of each industry's output devoted, directly or indirectly, to waste.

Table 2 shows the waste final demand vectors. The waste industries have been treated throughout as a final demand category so that total final demand in the model equals actual 1970 final demand plus the inputs to the waste industries. For comparison with the actual 1970 final demand levels waste industry inputs have therefore been excluded from both totals on the right hand side of the equation:

Productive Final Demand *equals*
Total Final Demand *minus* Waste Final Demand

4.

Results and Conclusions

Productive gross output summed over all industries came to 38·57 per cent of total gross output. This figure, while involving multiple counting of product shows the position in terms of ongoing activity, and indicates that of employment.

Productive final demand was 39·71 per cent of total final demand in 1970.

Table 2: Waste Final Demand by Industry, Distributed by Waste Category: US 1970

	Military	Federal government non-military	State and local government	Waste industry output	Investment in waste industry	Waste personal consumption	Consumption from business and property income	Total waste	Total final demand	Waste as % total final demand	Waste industry inputs
1 Agriculture	562·02	-109·00	-66·39	0·00	0·00	1592·97	945·66	2925·26	10526·60	27·79	3277·00
2 Metal mining	0·30	0·50	0·00	0·00	0·00	0·00	0·00	0·80	214·60	0·37	12·51
3 Coal, stone, et al.	108·07	14·60	36·11	0·00	0·00	229·35	189·85	577·98	2398·20	24·10	1119·20
4 Oil and gas	2071·95	27·70	228·04	0·00	0·00	350·74	2272·96	8251·39	15741·90	52·42	2247·90
5 Construction	1089·74	1088·78	3826·59	1296·23	5382·00	0·00	0·00	10263·33	72150·70	17·58	9036·10
6 Ordnance	5167·11	168·60	1·99	0·00	0·00	9·25	156·48	5586·43	6698·30	83·40	3·20
7 Food	5364·77	-11·90	120·73	0·00	0·00	18309·11	10869·91	34652·22	66702·90	51·95	3530·00
8 Tobacco	394·66	0·00	0·18	0·00	0·00	1617·32	68·23	2696·39	5805·30	46·45	204·50
9 Textiles, apparel	2066·65	21·50	46·14	0·00	0·00	7048·42	6193·80	15376·50	19090·30	80·55	555·50
10 Lumber, wood products	36·31	-14·20	1·27	0·00	0·00	79·12	41·81	144·31	538·20	26·81	563·00
11 Furniture	316·36	23·10	116·53	0·00	0·00	1119·769	929·29	2582·97	6216·90	41·55	82·40
12 Paper and products	149·53	36·80	3·26	0·00	0·00	452·94	502·29	1144·81	1876·30	61·01	1653·00
13 Printing, publishing	490·77	35·10	116·00	0·00	0·00	1279·70	974·62	2896·18	5619·00	51·54	1622·10
14 Chemicals, plastic	1134·34	68·50	232·75	0·00	0·00	2427·42	1588·07	5451·08	14210·30	38·36	10620·40
15 Rubber, leather	350·75	22·10	41·45	5300·82	0·00	850·14	942·78	2207·22	4085·90	54·02	961·40
16 Footwear	290·86	1·10	0·54	0·00	0·00	974·75	886·45	2154·00	3732·50	57·71	1237·50
17 Primary metal	120·05	39·00	29·67	0·00	0·00	15·38	11·84	186·81	2588·20	7·22	68·90
18 Fabricated metal	280·07	20·30	29·67	0·00	0·00	358·44	282·88	971·36	4461·40	21·77	1270·90
19 Non-electrical machinery	795·72	106·90	166·12	676·50	280·00	341·47	293·27	1703·48	28235·40	6·03	1561·30
20 Electrical equipment	6646·04	247·36	52·87	0·00	0·00	3463·04	2890·72	2823·54	4634·90	60·89	1622·10
21 Transport equipment	10236·15	241·39	241·14	0·00	1612·00	7411·39	5616·70	14356·54	23412·50	61·01	2066·69
22 Instruments	806·23	72·30	57·54	0·00	0·00	673·00	512·65	2121·71	6120·60	34·67	2919·64
23 Miscellaneous manufacture	413·28	5·10	108·60	0·00	0·00	1640·38	1249·27	3416·64	7396·50	46·19	655·20
24 Transportation, warehousing	3572·94	-28·90	213·76	0·00	0·00	4355·13	7074·85	15187·78	21043·90	72·17	865·60
25 Communications	1035·12	36·20	120·87	0·00	0·00	2807·64	856·12	4855·96	5688·90	85·36	5731·10
26 Utilities	1339·56	44·70	285·78	0·00	0·00	4507·29	238·10	6415·43	17036·90	37·66	7362·80
27 Trade	1898·35	10·43	17·25	9277·37	6743·00	703·48	5336·52	11383·54	18888·10	95·75	4510·20
28 Finance, insurance	0·00	0·00	0·00	22756·60	0·00	0·00	0·00	22756·60	22756·60	100·00	1360·49
29 Real estate	0·00	0·00	0·00	7640·90	0·00	0·00	0·00	7640·90	7640·90	100·00	0·00
30 Hotels, services	1366·90	20·50	53·87	11680·83	0·00	4250·07	2678·50	20050·66	20122·40	99·64	2183·80
31 Auto repair, services	393·01	4·29	44·88	1032·24	0·00	1599·93	971·10	4005·45	6471·70	61·89	1790·10
32 Amusements	387·93	2·20	-22·81	0·00	0·00	1195·13	480·18	2042·64	5006·30	40·80	477·50
33 Medical, educational, non-profit	3159·66	130·70	105·89	0·00	0·00	10981·36	3474·49	17842·10	37455·70	47·66	473·80
34 Miscellaneous	810·52	224·69	308·69	341·98	0·00	1055·47	557·71	3299·06	4344·50	75·94	5302·21
35 Imports	2752·16	194·60	3·26	0·00	0·00	2102·93	3567·07	8620·01	49800·00	17·21	689·90
Sum	55607·87	2832·04	6493·46	212265·46	14017·00	93553·46	63289·78	448047·07	743212·20	60·29	
% Total final demand	7·48	0·38	0·87	28·56	1·89	12·59	8·52	60·29			
% Total Waste	12·41	0·63	1·45	47·38	3·13	20·88	14·13	100·00			

Within the terms of the definitions developed in Part I, three-fifths of the work *actually undertaken* in the US in 1970 was wasted from capital's own point of view. This excludes the work that *might have been* undertaken were it not for unemployment: an average of four million in that year, or 4·9 per cent of the work force (say 12·5 per cent of the productive work force). It excludes the productive output lost through duplication, excessive seemingly-productive consumption, irrational ideologically-induced methods of work and so on. It excludes a view of the system from some other, historic, stand point. To repeat – it is a measure, cautiously estimated, of the waste that goes on inside the system. It does not measure the waste *of* the system. It is the measure capital itself would take of itself if only it could.

1. The most extensive work on the constituents of a productive economy are the analyses used by the military for targetting and survival exercises. These are not normally open to outsiders. Occasionally they surface. During World War II the American 'bedrock' programme unexpectedly came up for open discussion in Congress – a Congressman wanted to know why whisky production was included amongst essential industries. The programme itself was 'an estimate of the level of civilian end-product output at which war production would be at a maximum . . . above or below which the war effort would be weakened' (Harry B. Yoshpe, Charles F. Franke *et al.*, *Production for Defense*, Washington, DC: Industrial College of the Armed Forces 1968, p158. This is a National Security Management textbook). Since then the idea of a core economy has taken root. In the late fifties there was a great deal of discussion about burying a self-contained US sub-economy in underground shelters. One fervent advocate wrote:
'It is possible to determine within our present economy a sub-economy which provides at least a certain number of interdependent essential activities, free from all luxuries, all frills. It will secure the very barest *but continuing* existence of a part of the population – that part which may be assumed as saved by shelters or by-passed in a large-scale attack . . . The sub-economy must be a surplus-producing economy. . . . The sub-

economy . . . must form an integrated system which can live by itself. . . .

'The proper design of the sub-economy should not only accomplish the construction of an economy which can work by itself when the surface economy is knocked out or gravely wounded. It should be able to rebuild the country gradually from the remnants left over.' (Oskar Morgenstern, *The Question of National Defense*, 2nd revised edition, New York: Vintage Books 1961, pp130–1. Emphasis in original.)

An elaborate official study of such a core economy was started in the US Office of Emergency Planning in 1962. Called *Nuclear Attack Hazards in the Continental United States 1963* (NAHICUS 63) it was based on over 700,000 distinct resource points or resource records stored on tapes. Its aim was to ascertain the conditions for economic survival and recovery of a post-attack US reduced to one-quarter of the then current economic size. Amongst its subsidiary aims was the updating and refinement of the inter-industry input-output tables (on which this essay is based) in order, *inter alia*, to 'determine the final *essential* demand of . . . private consumption, Government expenditure, capital investment, and foreign export' (Charles Primoff, 'Balancing Resource Requirements Against Resource Capabilities', in Harry B. Yoshpe (ed), *Requirements: Matching Needs with Resources*, Washington DC: Industrial College of the Armed Forces 1964, p110, emphasis added).

2. In conventional national income accounting, gnp falls if well-heeled bachelors marry their housekeepers and rises if they then change their minds and buy revolvers to effect the change.

3. Unfortunately, we are not doing too well. To judge by recent writing on the subject, marxists in England at least, can be as obscure and ideological as any bourgeois academic, and as insensitive to the historic contexts in which their analytic categories were formed and are used The worst recent sinner in this respect is John Harrison who concludes that 'Marx's attempt to formulate a scientific category of unproductive labour employed by capital was fundamentally misconceived'; that 'all labour performed under the capitalist mode of production should be treated as "productive"'; and that 'all constant capital is "productive" constant capital'. Not even the most dyed-in-the-wool of the system's trusties would say that when sober. ('Productive and Unproductive Labour in Marx's Political Economy', *Bulletin of the Conference of Socialist Economists*, Autumn 1973, pp78, 81).

4. As Marx put it, 'that labourer alone is productive who produces surplus-value for the capitalist, and thus works for the self-expansion of capital' (*Capital*, Vol. I, Moscow, Foreign Languages Publishing House 1961, p509).

5. Cf. Marx, *Theories of Surplus Value*, 'the doctor who prescribes pills is not a productive labourer' (Vol. I, p180 of the Moscow edition, Foreign Languages Publishing House, nd); 'what the labourer . . . pays out for the services of physicians, lawyers, priests, is his misfortune' (*ibid.*, p205).

6. The teacher's case is ambiguous: 'a schoolmaster is a productive labourer when, in addition to belabouring the heads of his scholars, he works like a horse to enrich the school proprietor. That the latter has laid out his capital in a teaching factory, instead of in a sausage factory, does not alter the relation' (*Capital*, Vol. I, p509).

7. Cf. *Theories of Surplus Value*:

'When on the other hand the bourgeoisie has won the battle and has partly itself taken over the State, partly made a compromise with its former possessors and has likewise given recognition to the ideological professions as flesh of its flesh and everywhere transformed them into its functionaries, of like nature to itself; when it itself no longer confronts these as the representative of productive labour, but when the real productive labourers rise against it and moreover tell it that it lives on other people's industry; when it is enlightened enough not to be entirely absorbed in production, but to want also to consume "in an enlightened way"; when the spiritual labours themselves are more and more performed in its *service* and enter into the service of capitalist production – then things take a new turn, and the bourgeoisie tries to justify "economically", from its own standpoint, what at an earlier stage it had criticised and fought against. Its spokesmen and conscience-salvers in this line are the Garniers, etc. In addition to this, these economists, who themselves are priests, professors, etc., are eager to prove their "productive" usefulness, to justify their wages "economically" ' (Vol. I, p292).

8. This is a fairly common mistake. Cf. for example, Paul Mattick: 'Government-induced production can enlarge total social production; but it cannot enlarge the total capital' (*Marx and Keynes*, Boston: Extending Horizons Books 1969, p158).

9. John Harrison, *loc cit.* and 'The Political Economy of Housework', *Bulletin of the CSE*, Winter 1973.

10. Paul A. Baran, *The Political Economy of Growth*, New York: Monthly Review Press 1957, p32.

Baran continues: '*Most generally speaking [unproductive labour]
consists of all labor resulting in the output of goods and services
the demand for which is attributable to the specific conditions and
relationships of the capitalist system, and which would be absent
in a rationally ordered society*' (emphasis in original).

11. Marx assumed, in passing, that capitalists divide their
personal expenditure in the proportion of 'three-fifths for
necessities . . . and two-fifths for luxuries' (*Capital*, Vol. II
p404).

As between the two sub-branches producing necessities and
luxuries (Departments IIa and IIb), he wrote, 'a considerable
part of the instruments of labour as such, as well as of the raw
and auxiliary materials, etc., is the same for both departments'
(*Capital*, Vol. II, p407).

12. Joseph D. Phillips, 'Estimating the Economic Surplus', in
Paul A. Baran and Paul M. Sweezy, *Monopoly Capital*, New
York and London: Monthly Review Press 1966, p384 supra.

13. *Monthly Labor Review*, December 1971, pp3–11.

14. *Survey of Current Business*, July 1971, p30.

15. Stephen P. Dresch, Robert D. Goldberg and An-loh Lin,
The Economic Potential of Disarmament Alternatives. Preliminary
and Incomplete Draft for Department of Economic and
Social Affairs, United Nations, 27 July 1972 (cyclostyled).

16. 'Input-Output Structure of the US Economy: 1963', *Survey
of Current Business*, November 1969.

17. *Survey of Current Business*, July 1971, p30.

18. US data from *Survey of Current Business*, April 1965; data
for the USSR from *New Directions in the Soviet Economy*, studies
prepared for the Sub-Committee on Foreign Economic Policy
of Joint Economic Committee of the US Congress 89th Congress,
Second Session, Washington DC, 1966, Table A-1, p657
and Table A-1, p772.

19. *Survey of Current Business 1971*, and *Consumer Buying
Indicators*, US Department of Commerce, Series P-65, no 35,
May 1971.

20. See, for example, Phillips, *loc. cit.* pp381–4 and refs.

21. *Construction Review*, US Department of Commerce, Bureau
of Domestic Commerce, May 1971, p24.

22. *US Census of Population 1960*, Subject Report PC (2)–7.

23. Richard P. Oliver, 'Employment effect of reduced defense
spending', *Monthly Labor Review*, December 1971.

24. 'Income and Employment, by Industry', *Survey of Current
Business*, July 1971, p35.

25. *Survey of Current Business*, April 1971.

26. S.Cochran and D.P.Eldridge, 'Employment and Personal Consumption Expenditures', *Monthly Labor Review*, March 1972.

27. A.Soltow (ed), *Six Papers on the Size Distribution of Wealth and Income*, New York: National Bureau of Economic Research 1969, p128.

28. *Survey of Consumer Income and Expenditure for 1960–61* BLS Report no.237–93), US GPO February 1965, p11.

29. *Survey of Current Business*, April 1971.

30. From *Survey of Consumer Income and Expenditure, loc. cit.*

3. Marx's Theory of Value

> In theory it is assumed that the laws of capitalist pro-
> duction operate in their pure form. In reality there
> exists only approximation; but, this approximation is
> the greater, the more developed the capitalist mode
> of production and the less it is adulterated and amal-
> gamated with survivals of former economic condi-
> tions. (Marx)[1]

It seems improbable that marxists should have spent a
century defending two very abstract propositions: that values are
measured by the amount of time necessarily and actively spent in
creating them, and that under certain stringently-defined and
wholly artificial conditions equal values exchange. It is at least
as improbable that *anti*-marxists should have spent as much time
attacking them, or that a blander school of *non*-marxists should
now bother to deny their relevance. Yet in different tones and with
different talent, they have done so and, as this shows, are still
doing so.

I.

The Propositions

Like all societies capitalism manages to allocate its labour
and distribute its output more or less systematically. Alone

First published in *International Socialism* 32, Spring 1968.

amongst them it does so unintendingly, without overall planning. And it does so while sustaining an exceptionally fast rate of growth and despite intense and disruptive class struggle. However one looks at it, this is an extraordinary achievement.

Its explanation is the substance of classical political economy. Basic to it are the two propositions with which we started. And in the same way as the explanation at Marx's hands went well beyond capitalism's coherence and equilibrium to encompass its development and decay, so did the two standard propositions come to fulfil uncommonly explicit and important functions.

The first anchored his model of capitalism to historical materialism: it measured the achievements of this society, the extent of its mastery over the environment, on a scale common to all – the cost in socially significant human effort. The second fastened on the element of normalcy, regularity, law within the system, without which it could not persist. Together they articulated a model that featured the most significant relationships in capitalist society as its own.

Few of these relationships were Marx's discovery. Class struggle, accumulation, exploitation, expansion were attributed to the system before him, and without reference to him subsequently. What was new was his attempt to relate these known facts to each other systematically and above all quantitatively, and to do so in terms that both dealt in and rejected the categories used in justifying the system to its members, that is, critically.

Take class struggle. To say that labour power is a commodity, that is, useless to its owner unless exchanged, is not very significant in itself. To say that it must exchange at its value; that this value is measured by the amount of time necessarily and actively spent in its creation and renewal; that this amount of time is manifestly less than the duration for which labour power is bought; and that the difference is the measure of exploitation, or the time spent creating the flow of profits, rent, interest – is more than interesting. It puts class struggle in a social context. It provides a criterion for differentiating one type of income from another – income from work and income from 'property' (that is, from the exercise of social power). On a different plane, it explains the reality of inequality as well as the appearance of equal rights; the realities of dependence and compulsion as well as the appearance of contractual freedom.

Or take accumulation and growth. The time necessary and actively spent in production – Marx's 'socially necessary labour time' – is contingent on technology and its application. Neither being evenly spread through the economy, there is a gap between what is individually- and what is socially-necessary, between individual and normal productivity. In its positive aspect, this gap is the source of above average profits. To exploit it by using 'shadow', normal costs instead of actual, individual costs, and to widen it by innovation, speedup, or whatever, become through competition the operational goals of each capital. That they are paradoxical and ultimately self-defeating goals is true: above-average profits derive from a successful bid to push back the sway of ruling normal costs, while these costs are themselves established through the normalization and socialization of the special circumstances which make above-average profits possible. They are none the less compulsive for that; and their effect is to be seen in the dynamism of the capitalist economy, in the fact that growth is a condition of its existence.

In both cases – and they are representative – the facts are seldom disputed. Even their configuration might be allowed. What is never conceded is that they are linked and consistent with the two quantitative propositions on which Marx's value theory rests. To do so would be to concede the ism as well as the man.

2.
The 'Reduction Problem'

For a century or so neither proposition has gained much of a hearing outside the socialist tradition. The first – value is measured by the time actively and necessarily spent in its creation, by 'socially necessary labour time' – has been rejected on a number of grounds, the most important being that labour is not homogeneous and cannot be reduced to 'simple, average labour', that is to 'the expenditure of simple labour-power, . . . labour-power which, on an average, apart from any special development, exists in the organism of every ordinary individual.'[2]

One critic saw 'this problem [as] certainly the most serious difficulty met by an inherent criticism of Marxist economics' and one without solution.[3] Others, from Böhm-Bawerk[4] through Bernstein[5] down to Joan Robinson[6] have picked on it as a crucial weakness.

Marx himself did not give it much attention. He thought it enough to state that 'the different proportions in which different sorts of labour are reduced to unskilled labour as their standard, are established by a social process that goes on behind the backs of the producers, and, consequently, appear to be fixed by custom';[7] that the social process in question was one of enriching simple skills through education and upbringing which 'costs an equivalent in commodities of a greater or less amount';[8] and that the use of these enriched skills produces 'labour of a higher class, labour that creates in equal times proportionally higher values than unskilled labour does.'[9] He saw the level of skills as something analogous to the organic composition of capital and the use of skilled labour in production as analogous to the transfer of accumulated labour (constant capital) to the product, with one crucial difference, that in the latter case there is a simple *transfer* of value and in the former not.

Marx let the matter remain even vaguer than the analogy implies. He spent little time on justifying *unskilled* labour time as the measure of value: it was enough that 'unskilled labour constitutes the bulk of all labour performed in capitalist society.'[10] There seemed no reason to be more explicit, for at the time to reduce skilled to simple labour was to distil in theory a real and clearly noticeable social process in which the predominant skills (in agriculture and handicrafts) were being ruined; the use of undifferentiated, unskilled labour was growing explosively; and the social nature of individual labour, its role in the total division of labour, was being reaffirmed daily as a wholly external fact, embodied in machinery and in the organizing will of capital. If the problem of reduction obtruded it was because skilled wages were so disproportionate to the going rate for simple labour; if it was thought to be fairly unimportant nonetheless it was because newly-employed skills were still relatively few.

Times changed. Under pressure from the critics and from the growing mass, variety and definition in the skills used by capital, marxists laboured to refine the original statement. Hilferding's formulation of 1904 has remained more or less the stock answer to this day. As he put it,

> For the production of . . . skilled labour power . . . a number of unskilled labours [are] requisite . . .
> Its expenditure consequently signifies the expenditure of all the different unskilled labours which are simultaneously condensed therein . . .
> In what it has to give for the product of skilled labour, society consequently pays an equivalent for the value which the unskilled labours would have created had they been directly consumed by society. [Of course,] a skilled labour may contain, not unskilled labours alone, but in addition skilled labours of a different kind, [but] these in their turn are reducible to unskilled labour.'[11]

Although echoed since by most marxist writers on the subject,[12] it is an unsatisfactory answer. In the actual process of education as it takes place in schools, at the apprentice's bench or at home, the labour used in creating skills is itself skilled labour by and large, which in turn owes its provenance to the input of skills and so on through the reaches of time past. This must always have been true – enough at least to justify Marx's perfunctoriness about the reduction process – but never more than today when manual labour is typically skilled or semi-skilled, and unskilled labour however defined (and most definitions include a skill component) forms only a fifth or so of the whole.[13]

It would satisfy one's sense of history and of aptness if *skilled* labour time could be substituted as the measure of value. It would also simplify the arithmetic, since a narrowing of differentials always accompanies a general enrichment with skills.[14] But skills are nothing if not concrete, and nothing concrete can serve as a general measure of value. For if it is difficult to translate the value of, say, an electrician's labour power into that of a labourer's, even though all electricians can work as labourers, it is impossible to effect the translation as between an electrician and, say, an engineering fitter. Neither exercises that 'labour-power which, on an average, apart from any special development, exists in the organism of every ordinary individual.' Each is immobilized by the other's particular concrete skill.

In fine, while skilled labour is *representative* where unskilled labour is now not, it lacks the *universalism* which unskilled labour still has. A measure of value needs both.

In Marx's day the two combined naturally in unskilled labour. It was the typical form of labour – and so representative; it was functionally subordinated to capital, socialized so to speak only at work, to which it brought no more than brute force – and so universal. Today labour's functional subordination to capital is more total; integration and socialization occur as much off the job as on it – in education, in leisure, via the media; it brings to work specialism, functional immobility, the need to combine in fairly fixed proportions not only with external capital but with itself. If, therefore, in Marx's day the social character of labour could be represented by an individual labour power, today it cannot. What is employed now is a composite, a blending of individual skills into a collective unit, which, although unrecognized in theory, exists in practice as the recipient of collective bonuses, the product of industrial training schemes, of educational efforts or of recruiting drives. In effect, it is what moves between industries.

There is nothing abhorrent to Marx's method in this. On the contrary: in order to eliminate random differences in the work intensity and inherent skill of individual workers, he posited an 'average social labour' which resulted 'whenever a certain minimum number of workmen are employed together.'[15] In another connexion he posited an 'average capital' (with 'the same, or approximately the same structure as the average social capital') as a limit towards which 'all other capitals, of whatever composition, tend.'[16] A composite labour power, weighted in accordance with the skill composition of the total social labour force – a standard composite, as it were – is of the same genre.

Its use does not 'solve' the reduction problem. The blend of skills in each industry is unlikely to coincide with that of the standard composite, and some sort of reduction process – from non-standard to standard composites – is still needed. But since industries and, more particularly, the large capitals that straddle them share a narrower range of composites than the range of individual skills within them; and since the range of composites narrows as the composition of capitals becomes increasingly uniform (as will be shown in Section 4 below), the problem is reduced in importance and tends to disappear in practice. At the same time the measure of value is shifted from the individual to the collective plane where it obviously now belongs.

3.
A Methodological Interlude

A more general objection, which, if upheld, would destroy the argument not only in Section 2 but throughout this article, is that it is pointless to seek empirical evidence for Marx's categories. He was, after all dealing with the 'reality behind the reality', the essence beneath the surface of phenomena. In this view, occasionally, if furtively, held by contributors to this journal, it does not matter at all if the concept 'simple labour' (or 'value', or 'surplus value' presumably) has an objective correlative; importance attaches only to the coherence of the model that requires the concept and to its ability to illumine reality whether or no it mirrors it.

It can be admitted at once that no model mirrors reality in all its detail: scaling down – the building of the model – is a process of exclusion and simplification, and scaling up again – the model's use – replaces the original rich texture of uniqueness with flat expanses of generalization and abstraction. So much is true. What is *untrue*, is that the process of scaling down can produce categories that have no objective correlative; or that in the contrary process of scaling up features essential to the model can be made to disappear. To suppose anything else is to justify the use of ideas as a pure convenience.

Marx was aware of the need to root his categories in reality. Paradoxically, *Capital* is at its most empirical when dealing with the larger abstractions – as in volume I. The subsequent two volumes, in which successively closer approximations are made to the actual functioning of the system, are by contrast almost devoid of factual material. No doubt this is partly due to the fact that Marx did not prepare the published text himself; but mostly, as can be seen from Engels' Introductions, it is because there was so little. Presumably Marx felt it more important to anchor a grand generalization in experience, than a small one. 'Abstract labour' or 'labour in general' was one of the grandest. Yet it 'has found its highest development in the most modern of bourgeois societies, the United States.'[17] The reduction process was another. Yet, although it 'appears to be an abstraction . . . it is an abstraction which takes place daily in the social process of production.'[18] If it is 'British empiricism' to appeal outside the model in justifying its categories, Marx, despite his accent, despite his philosophy and despite his own protestations, was a 'British empiricist' of a high order.

4.

The 'Transformation Problem'

The need for verification sustained the longest, most exhaustive and boring of the debates on the Labour Theory, relating to its second proposition – that value equivalents exchange.

In the first volume of *Capital*, Marx conveniently assumed that capital and labour-power combined in a fixed value proportion – the organic composition of capital was given; that labour-power was used at the same intensity and for the same length of time in all cases – the rate of surplus value, or exploitation, was given; and that, as a result, surplus value accrued to capital in proportion to its size – the rate of profit was everywhere the same. Prices therefore equalled values and the proposition about value equivalents exchanging presented no difficulty.

In volume III, one of these restrictive assumptions was dropped: the rate of exploitation was still held constant, but capital and labour-power were allowed, as realism demands, to combine in different value proportions. One of two conclusions had now to be drawn: either the rate of profit on different capitals varied in line with their organic compositions and prices coincided with values – which was manifestly not the case, nor could be so long as capital was free to move from less to more profitable spheres; or prices diverged from values in such a way as to more or less equalize profit rates. Obviously this was what was happening. Equally obviously, the systematic divergence demanded clarification.

Marx set about the problem in part II of the third volume of *Capital*. Essentially what he did was to aggregate separate capitals into one social capital and redistribute the total profit (equal to the total surplus value) among the capital components in proportion to their size. For an individual capital, total revenue (price of production) would then be equal to cost price (that is, depreciation on fixed capital and outlay on circulating capital and wages) plus its share of total profit, or cost price plus the average rate of profit. A capital of low organic composition (relatively labour intensive) would receive a revenue below the value of its product; a capital of high organic composition (relatively capital intensive) would price its products above their value. Not to do so would be to induce a congestion of capital and low profits in labour-intensive sectors, scarcity of capital and high profits in capital-intensive ones, with consequent redistribution of investment until each capital was satisfied that it was receiving the ruling rate of profit.

Marx illustrated his argument with a minimum of fuss. He was interested in showing that values *can* be transformed into prices, that the exchange of value-equivalents on which his theories of exploitation and surplus value rested, although modified, still held – and this he did.

The illustration was not intended as proof. In particular, he explicitly abstracted from the complications introduced by different capitals' use of each others' outputs as inputs[19] and so accomplished only half the 'transformation' required: in effect, each capital's output was 'priced' but its inputs were 'valued.' The formal problem thus remained: to find a ratio of price to value, whether a commodity was considered as output or input, that would ensure a rate of profit common to all capitals. The critics naturally thought this impossible; nor was the immediate defense too productive. It was left to latterday Ricardians, Ladislaus von Bortkiewicz, a statistician at Berlin University in the first third of the century, and, implicitly, Piero Sraffa, editor of Ricardo's *Works* at Cambridge, to open and decisively close the solution.

There is no point in tracing their arguments here. It is enough to say that Bortkiewicz constructed a determinate equational system (in which the number of unknowns was no more than the number of equations) from Marx's conditions of equilibrium as set out in part III of the second volume of *Capital* and so arrived at a formally satisfactory solution;[20] and that Sraffa, in an ambitious and formidable work, *Production of Commodites by Means of Commodities*, showed there to be one set of price ratios for every fractional breakdown of output between wages and profits.[21] Marx has been vindicated, even if not by marxists.

While economists have puzzled over the 'transformation problem,' investing it with an importance never intended, reality has moved in an opposite direction – towards an increasing uniformity of organic compositions in different industries. This was to be expected on general grounds. As Marx points out, 'at first, capital subordinates labour on the basis of the technical conditions in which it historically finds it. It does not, therefore, change immediately the mode of production.'[22] Ultimately, however, it does; at first haphazardly as technical innovation occurs now in one, then in another industry, in response to market pressures or pure chance. Then more systematically as innovation and with it the deepening of industry's capital structure – the raising of its organic composition – becomes the organized output of research and development teams, themselves the planned product of national educational apparatuses. In this process the most traditional, labour-intensive industries have farthest to go and make the greatest relative progress.

Empirical backing is not easy to find. The ruling schools of economics have no use for capital:labour (value) ratios and spend no time elaborating them from the raw data to be found in censuses of production; marxist economics is denied the resources of orthodoxy which would make such elaboration possible. Nonetheless, what meagre evidence exists supports the thesis that these ratios (if only in their bastard form – capital [value]:labour [quantity]) are converging and that, more directly, the range, or dispersal, of industry organic compositions in this form is narrowing remarkably quickly.

On the first point, the fact of convergence – of fourteen British industries ordered by relative capital:labour ratios (in the above sense) in 1961, five of the first seven showed a lower than average rate of growth in this ratio between 1948 and 1964 and four of the bottom seven – an above average increase.[23] On the second point – the speed of convergence – it is possible to show that the dispersal of US industries, as represented by the five hundred largest firms, around the median, as represented by assets per employee, fell by more than two-fifths between 1960 and 1967; or, more rigorously, the coefficent of variation from the median fell from 75·4 to 43·0 in those eight years.[24]

It would be wrong to suggest that Marx's volume I assumption of a single organic composition of capital was intended as anything more than an expository device. It would be as wrong, however, to assert – as Sweezy does – that there is 'no justification [for it] in actual tendencies at work in a competitive capitalist economy'; or that 'there is obviously nothing to bring the ratios of constant to variable capital in the steel and clothing industries into conformity': and that it is this unreality which distinguishes it from others of Marx's propositions, such as the tendency of profit rates towards equality. On the contrary, the growth in scale of manufacturing, its increasing technological intensity, the increasing organization and planning of research, all on a background of labour shortage and compulsive economic growth, are in fact prodding the steel and clothing industries into conformity, as they are prodding reality closer to Marx's proposition.[25]

5.

Supersession by Planning ?

The 'non'-marxist critique spares itself the pain of wrestling with Marx's own categories: they were useful in his time but irrelevant today. Marx should rest embalmed in his own distinction, and be ignored except in as much as he has been pacified and annexed.

One variant originated with the debate on value theory in post-revolutionary Russia. It is still reverberating through the non-Chinese eastern bloc and has even found a sophisticated echo in non-Stalinist circles in the West. It states simply that planning and the Law of Value (in its 'exchange of equivalents' aspect) are diametrically opposed and mutually exclusive principles of economic organization; the one denies existence to the other. In its refined, academic version it states, less simply, that since understanding, intention and behaviour are inseparable, social 'laws' as distinct from physical ones lose their compelling character through being formulated; that Marx, by revealing the principles by which capitalism organizes itself, effectively annulled them. At its most sophisticated, this view would agree with Marx in denying explicitly an identity between formulating a social 'law' and its supersession, between recognition and annulment;[26] would admit that between the one and the other an institutional bridge need be built; but would say, so it has been, or is being, built – from Russia to the United States planning is respectable, needs are foreseen, catered for, and the 'common mind' of the 'agents of production' which Marx would not or could not envisage as reality, is to be found in the planning commissions or their equivalents in every capital city.

In a sense they are right. The evidence of planning is plain. But the evidence has always been there. There has always been a measure of planning under capitalism and the picture today is very little different – scale for scale – from what it was in Marx's day. What the critics have done is present a false disjunction between the Law of Value and planning; between compulsion and choice; necessity and freedom. Under capitalism, the antonyms are and always have been inseparable; individual capitals have always attempted to evade the full consequences of planlessness by extending their own sphere of control. Their growth as a result has always resulted in even greater anarchy.

Marx was explicit and repetitive on this: 'in a society with capitalist production,' he concluded 'anarchy in the social division of labour and despotism in that of the workshop are mutual conditions the one of the other.'[27] Others, from an intellectual tradition more congenial to the agnostic critics, have taken a narrower view, but are emphatic enough: 'the development of the modern business enterprise can be understood only as a comprehensive effort to reduce risk. It is not going too far to say that it can be understood in no other terms.'[28]

Nor can it. At the very least, capital must see that its outlay on labour-power, raw materials and so on is no more than at ruling prices; and that they are employed at the prevailing standards of efficiency. Anything less would result in a lower than average rate of profit, a relative decline in competitive ability and ultimate extinction. Anything more, however, results in setting new standards for productivity, for the 'socially necessary labour time', that other capitals must in the end adopt. The imposition of these new standards, as the preservation of the old, is the foundation of despotic planning. In other words, the transformation of competition's planlessness into planning is the specific function of capital, the ruling class's only justification. And if the

attempt to limit the effect of planlessness results in expanding the
area of planning – through accumulation, concentration, the
formation of monopolies, trusts, cartels and even national capital
units – this is no proof of anarchy's supercession but of its displacement.

To prove supercession, the critics need to show that the
relations between individual capitals are determined *a priori*. This
they can still do for the state capitalist countries. Even in Yugoslavia, the most 'devolved' and 'reformed' of them all, 'the government uses various market instruments in order to make the Social
Plan workable and efficient and to attain planned goals.'[29] In the
countries of orthodox capitalism, the thesis would be more difficult
to prove, but at least it is arguable within each national state. But
internationally the system still forms in the classic capitalist
manner – there is no goal, no *a priori* purpose, no fundamental
check to the spontaneity of competition. Final authority is dispersed over a number of independent governments, each important enough for its decisions to be crucial to those of all the others
yet each taking its decisions independently and privately, and so
with inherently unforeseeable consequences. The resulting extreme vulnerability of each to all leads to consistent attempts to
speed up national responses to international economic events, that
is to plan and centralize economic control in each national centre.
Planning is reactive, not autonomous.

Such planning breeds planning. A product of international integration and competition, it destroys the automatism
of international adjustment – pure in theory, less so but still
there in practice – and the world market becomes an increasingly
unstable environment, demanding faster national adjustment,
increasing national articulation and so more planning. The distinction between the national economy in which competition is
heteronomous, one method of attaining goals set by international
competition, and the international economy where primordial
competition still holds, grows sharper and sharper.

Naturally attempts are made to order the international environment, to plan the planning: the wilful or inexpert use of the policy discretion now available to each national capital is potentially so dangerous to the rest that intense diplomatic pressure – backed by the threat of financial and political sanctions – is brought to bear to compel the adoption of particular policies. But the results are neither lasting nor universal. If nothing else, the level of world spending on armaments is witness to their limitations.

Capitalism is still a competitive system; and the law of value still the basis for its analysis.

1. *Capital*, Moscow: Foreign Languages Publishing House 1961–62, Vol. III, p172.
2. *Capital*, Vol. I, p44.
3. Rudolph Schlesinger, *Marx, His Time and Ours*, London: Routledge & Kegan Paul 1950, p129.
4. Eugen von Böhm-Bawerk, 'Karl Marx and the Close of his System', in Böhm-Bawerk, *Karl Marx etc.* and Rudolf Hilferding, *Böhm-Bawerk's Criticism of Marx*, edited with an introduction by Paul M. Sweezy, New York: Augustus M. Kelly 1949, pp81 ff.
5. Eduard Bernstein, 'On the Meaning of the Marxist Theory of Value' in *Evolutionary Socialism*, London: ILP 1909.
6. Joan Robinson, *Economic Philosophy*, Penguin, 1964, p44.
7. *Capital*, Vol. I, p44.
8. ibid. p172.
9. ibid. p197.
10. *A Contribution to the Critique of Political Economy*, Calcutta: Bharati Library (nd), p25. (Henceforth *Critique*.)
11. Rudolf Hilferding, *op. cit.*, pp144–6.
12. A post-war crop would include Paul M. Sweezy, *The Theory of Capitalist Development*, London: Dennis Dobson 1946, pp42–4; Ronald L. Meek, *Studies in the Labour Theory of Value*, London: Lawrence & Wishart 1956, pp172–3; Ernest Mandel, *Traité d'économie marxiste*, Paris: Julliard 1962, Vol. I, p78.
13. See Guy Routh, *Occupation and Pay in Great Britain, 1906–1960*, Cambridge University Press 1965, pp3–6, 42.

14. See *ibid.* pp.53–9, *passim* for figures covering this century in Britain.

15. *Capital*, Vol. I, pp323–4.

16. *Capital*, Vol. III, p171.

17. *Critique*, p299.

18. *ibid.*, p24.

19. 'There is always the possibility of an error if the cost-price of a commodity . . . is identified with the value of the means of production consumed by it. Our present analysis does not necessitate a closer examination of this point.' (*Capital*, Vol. III, p162.)

20. Bortkiewicz's major article on the subject, 'On the Correction of Marx's Fundamental Theoretical Construction in the Third Volume of *Capital*,' was originally published in 1907. Translated by Sweezy, it forms an Appendix to his edition of the Böhm-Bawerk/Hilferding debate, *op. cit.*

21. Cambridge University Press 1960. Its high level of abstraction is as responsible as the low level of current marxist scholarship for Sraffa's neglect. An appeal to Maurice Dobb and, indirectly, to Sraffa himself, elicited a total of five extended reviews from a marxist standpoint and one assessment in the five years following publication of his book.

A bibliography of English-language attempts at a solution of the 'transformation problem' in the period between Bortkiewicz and Sraffa can be found in Ronald L. Meek, 'Some Notes on the "Transformation Problem",' reprinted in *Economics and Ideology and Other Essays*, London: Chapman & Hall 1967, p143.

22. *Capital*, Vol. I, p310. The observation recurs a great number of times.

23. R.J.Nicholson, 'Capital Stock, Employment and Output in British Industry 1948–1964,' *Yorkshire Bulletin of Economic and Social Research*, November 1966, Table 3, p81.

24. *Fortune*, 'Directory of the Five Hundred Largest US Corporations,' mid-July issue of respective years.

25. If the textile industry might stand for Sweezy's 'clothing industry', and metal manufacturing for steel, the ratio of assets per employee in the two industries declined from 1:2.1 to 1:1.5 between 1959 and 1967. (From *Fortune*, *loc. cit.*)

26. Cf. Marx: 'The determination of the magnitude of value by labour-time is therefore a secret, hidden under the apparent fluctuations in the relative values of commodities. Its discovery . . . in no way alters the mode in which that determination takes place.' (*Capital*, Vol. I, p75, and *passim*.)

27. *Capital*, Vol. I, p356. See the entire section: 'Division of Labour in Manufacture, and Division of Labour in Society'.
28. John Kenneth Galbraith, *The Affluent Society*, Penguin 1962, p91.
29. Svetozar Pejovich, *The Market-Planned Economy of Yugoslavia*, Minneapolis, University of Minnesota Press 1966, p56.

4. Maginot Marxism: Mandel's Economics

Mandel's *Economics*[1] is a marxist failure. It is unsure of the central capitalist dynamic. It evades the essentials of the system as it operates today. It is more concerned with defending Marx's categories of analysis than with applying them. In consequence, it does little damage to the system intellectually or, by derivation, in practice.

I.

The Central Dynamic

If capitalism is peculiar among class societies, it is not because a surplus product is systematically pumped from the mass of producers – this happens in any class society – nor because a small section of society – the ruling class – organizes that pumping and benefits from it – that too happens in any class society – but because there is no central, public arrangement to ensure that the process will go on in an orderly, continuous and predictable way. Key choices about the deployment of resources are left to individual capitals, big and small, public and private.

Within nation states the doctrine of *ultra vires* holds,

First published in *International Socialism* 36, April/May 1969.

permitting individual capitals to do anything not expressly forbidden by laws whose scope and content they themselves determine to a large extent. Beyond, in the world shared between national capitals or the states with which they are more or less identified, positive constraints scarcely exist. Not even the largest state is coextensive with the system, so there are no overriding institutions that can make binding decision for it. Yet a sort of order emerges from the chaos.

That it does so is because the behaviour of individual capitals is narrowly determined by the competition between them. Simply in order to exist over any length of time each capital must grow as fast as it possibly can, by reinvesting the major part of its share of surplus-value (accumulation) or by absorbing and taking over other, less successful capitals (centralization), or by doing both. If an individual capital did not grow, it would ultimately be unable to afford the rationalization and innovation with which to meet those that did, or unable to ride as successfully the sudden changes in market conditions which are part of the system. For an individual capital growth is the ultimate compulsion.

Growth does not come about automatically. Since capital is not a being but a systematic relationship between beings, somebody has to decide to make growth happen, to devote the freely-disposable resources as they become available to investment rather than consumption. That somebody, whether an individual or a group, must be able to measure its performance against very clear criteria. It must also be very strongly motivated to make the right decisions, for primordial Adam has still not been gorged, not even by affluent late capitalism.

The precise forms these criteria and incentives take are unimportant. Historically the former have been as different as the amount of money profits and the volume of gross physical output; and the latter as different as material privilege or superior status at one end of the spectrum, and material loss or physical punishment at the other. What is important is that the criteria measure consistently the contribution of an individual's, or group's, decisions to the growth of any single capital; and that the incentives elicit as consistently the decisions that promote such growth.

This distinction between the behaviour of capital and the social and psychological mechanisms which ensure that behaviour, between the rules and the players of the game as it were, is obscured. It is nonetheless real, and of prime importance analytically. For the behaviour of capital – its blind unconcerted compulsion to grow – derives directly from the central peculiarity of the system – its fragmentation into more or less autonomous competing units – while the mechanisms whereby the ruling class organizes itself to promote that behaviour do not. These are common to all class societies.

The distinction does not exist for Mandel. On one page he concedes 'the *accumulation of capital*' as 'the great driving force of capitalist society'.[2] On another it is 'the capitalists' thirst for profit';[3] and on yet another money is 'the initial and final form of capital towards which the whole of economic activity is directed'.[4]

2.

The Essential Model

The primacy of growth is essential to Marx's model of the system at work. Each capital is driven to jack up productivity by coupling its workers with more, and more costly, machinery, while simultaneously trying to hold down wages. As this rationalization spreads, labour power becomes a smaller component of total capital (the 'organic composition of capital' rises) and smaller even in absolute terms (the 'reserve army of labour' grows); the value added in production and surplus value become smaller in relation to total investment; and so the average rate of profit falls. Booms become progressively less profitable and shorter;

FCT

slumps more lasting and severe. Stagnation threatens and the system becomes increasingly restrictive.

The model is a closed system, in which all output flows back as inputs in the form of investment goods or of wage goods. There are no leaks.

Yet in principle a leak could insulate the compulsion to grow from its most important consequences. If 'labour-intensive' goods were systematically drawn off, the overall organic composition of capital would rise faster than in a closed system. However, if 'capital-intensive' goods were drawn off, the rise would be slower and – depending on the volume and composition of the leak – could even stop or be reversed. In such a case there would be no decline in the averate rate of profit, no reason to expect increasingly severe slumps, and so on.

Capitalism has never formed a closed system in practice. Wars and slumps have destroyed immense quantities of output. Capital exports have diverted and frozen other quantities for long stretches of time.

A lot has, since World War II, filtered out in the production of arms. Each of these leaks has acted to slow the rise in the overall organic composition and the fall in the rate of profit. But since their size and composition have been spontaneously arrived at and not tailored to attaining these results their impact at any given time has been unpredictable except in broadest outline.

3.

The Historical Perspective

Arms production has clearly provided the largest and most effective normal drain since the second world war. Being a 'capital-intensive' drain it will have had a restraining effect on the tendency of the organic composition to rise. Without separating out the organic composition of the arms-producing industries and firms from that of the non-arms-producing ones and then carrying the exercise through all the backward linkages to their suppliers, their suppliers' suppliers and so on – an exercise which has yet to be undertaken – there is no way of measuring the effect directly, but it must have been considerable. For the expected immediate consequence of a rising organic composition, namely a fall in the average rate of profit, has not occurred. If us figures are any guide, the rate of profit has kept more or less level for the entire post-war period, as the accompanying table shows.

us: Corporate Profits before Tax and Net Working Capital, 1948–67

Year	Pre-tax profits	Net working capital	Profit rate
	$ billion	$ billion	$ billion
1948	32·7	68·6	47·7
1949	26·2	72·4	36·2
1950	40·0	81·6	49·0
1951	41·2	86·5	47·6
1952	35·9	90·1	39·8
1953	37·0	91·8	40·3
1954	33·2	95·0	34·9
1955	44·9	102·9	43·6
1956	44·7	107·4	41·6
1957	43·2	111·6	38·7
1958	37·4	118·7	31·5
1959	47·7	124·2	38·4
1960	44·3	128·6	34·4
1961	50·3	148·8	33·8
1962	55·4	155·6	35·6
1963	59·4	163·5	36·3
1964	66·8	170·0	39·3
1965	77·8	180·1	43·2
1966	85·6	189·4	45·2
1967	81·6	200·1	40·8

From *Federal Reserve Bulletin*, relevant years

There having been no long-term slide in profit rates, there has also not been a series of ever-deepening slumps or signs of growing restrictiveness. In fact output has seldom fallen from one year to the next since the war and then never by more than 2 per cent, and the tendency throughout the system has been *generally* away from inconvertibility, tariff barriers, resale price maintenance and so on. Nor has there been a steady increase in unemployment. Despite the evidence that has accumulated this last year or so of growing instability, the system has been kept open.

Mandel will have none of this. He does not so much as hint at the stringency of Marx's assumptions or at the extreme abstraction and simplicity of *Capital*'s theoretical construct. Marx said, therefore it must be. Models turn into the real thing; and the real thing becomes as simple as the model.

We are told, quite rightly, that 'increasing organic composition of capital . . . is the basic tendency of the capitalist mode of production'.[5] But then tendency is assumed to be fact and the next tendency in Marx's logical sequence – that of the average rate of profit to fall – is quickly tagged on as fact too: one table shows it to have dropped by two-fifths between 1889 and 1919;[6] another that net accumulation of capital fell catastrophically between the 1860s and the 1930s;[7] and two others that, depreciation has claimed more and more of gross output between the 1880s and the 1920s and between the 1880s and the 1940s (to 1948).[8] Since nothing beyond the forties could sustain Mandel's thesis, the facts are suspended then.

On to 'the inevitable slump'. Since the key fact here – the mildness of post-war recessions – is too public and obtrusive to be suppressed, it is conceded and even explained.[9] But, incredibly, it is not allowed to affect the larger analysis: the elusive inevitability is still announced at regular intervals;[10] slumps still punctuate a trend towards stagnation.[11] The uncomfortable fact is attached not incorporated.

The same is true of the drive to restrictiveness, immobility and decay. One by one they come: the 'absence of fresh fields for investment'[12] (as if interest rates were not constantly pressing upwards to attract scarce money capital, or were not now at a historically high level); the decline in trade relative to production[13] (as if trade in manufactures has not gone up at twice the rate of output since 1948);[14] the growth in the rentier class[15] (as if it has not been nearly euthanased since World War II by the combination of high profit retentions and high personal taxation); the march of cartelization in Britain[16] (as if competition for and from world markets were not increasing, or Resale Price Maintenance were still with us). There is even the quaint assertion, based on a crude misunderstanding of what insurance is about, that 'the chief preoccupation (of the capitalist regime) has become *security*, that is, conservation, and is no longer *expansion*'.[17]

But since this sort of statement and others about 'monopoly capitalism' limiting and fettering 'the development of the productive forces' look hairless even to Mandel, we are given a sop: it 'does not mean that world production, or even that of the leading countries, sinks into stagnation; but it falls even further short of the possibilities offered by modern techniques'.[18]

But once again, the admission is not allowed to affect the argument. The magpie goes gathering on, and we are left wondering what to make of non-stagnating stagnation, slumpless slumps and similar Mandelania.

4.

State Capitalism

Nothing in Stalinist (including post-Stalin) Russia defies analysis in terms of Marx's model. The process of pumping out surpluses from the mass of producers is as vulnerable in Russia to wild and random encroachments from other capitals as it is anywhere else. The people who organize and benefit from it, are under as oppressive a compulsion to fast economic growth as is any similarly placed class elsewhere. They need to be as clearly motivated to ensure growth as their counterparts abroad; and if their criterion of success has been the volume of gross physical output rather than money profits, the distinction is one of detail not essence – output has served the bureaucracy perfectly well as a success indicator, at least until very recently.

Some of these signals do get through. Mandel does concede that the deployment of resources in Russia is determined by its competitive relations with the outside world. As he puts it:

> International competition with capitalist economy also necessitated an increased shift of emphasis to the quality of products, the productivity of labour and the rationalization of investment, the volume of which moreover necessitated the maintenance of a high rate of growth even on the purely quantitative plane.[19]

He even recognizes that with an 'excessive rate of accumulation . . . the bureaucracy becomes the regulator and chief (sic) director of accumulation',[20] that the 'central political, economic and military administration' has exclusive 'controlling power over the social surplus product',[21] and that the 'Soviet leaders' 'deliberately chose to base themselves on the interests of privileged minorities rather than those of the mass of the workers, in order to give the necessary impetus to industrialization'.[22]

Typically, none of this means anything in terms of the analysis as a whole. Within fourteen pages of reading that 'international competition' determines the 'emphasis . . . on quality . . . productivity . . . rationalization . . . high rate of growth', determines in other words the content of the Plans, we are told that on the contrary, 'Soviet planning . . . is real planning, in so far as the totality of industrial means of production is in the hands of the state, which can thus centrally decide the level and rate of growth of production and accumulation.'[23] In even less space we make the transition from a bureaucracy organized as 'regulator and . . . director of accumulation', which is nothing if not a productive role, to a bureaucracy whose key characteristic is 'bourgeois norms of distribution'.

Part of this sloppiness derives from Mandel's original confusion about capitalism. Part from his determination to cast Russia as a 'transitional' society, neither capitalist nor yet socialist, a *'contradictory combination of a non-capitalist mode of production and a still basically bourgeois mode of distribution'*.[24]

Russia is not capitalist, he writes, because the bureaucrat is not 'subject to the tyranny of profit',[25] (true, the tyranny is of plan fulfilment); because there is no tendency for the rate of profit to fall (untrue, the tendency is there but checked as in the West); because there is no internal competition nor unimpeded operation of the law of value (true, nor is there – by definition – within any single capital); no flow of capital from low-productivity to high-productivity sectors (untrue, how else do the planners ensure growth); little exporting of capital to backward countries (true, but there is little of that from the West too); no overproduction (untrue, Mandel himself draws attention to the billions of rubles of unsold retail stocks of unwanted, socially unnecessary consumer goods);[26] no bourgeoisie (true, but a bureaucracy with – remember – 'controlling power over the social surplus product'); no free contractual relations between enterprises (less true as economic reform embraces a growing part of industry); no crisis (true, but not highly significant given the situation in the West). And so on.

But Russia is not socialist either: there is 'extensive social-inequality, bureaucratic privilege, lack of self-determination for the producers, etc.'[27] For, you see, 'the Bolshevik Party did not understand in good time the seriousness of this problem (of bureaucratic management), despite the many warnings sounded by Lenin and by the Left Opposition'![28]

So Russia is transitional. But what is a transitional society in Mandel's context other than a verbal convenience? Is such a form possible between capitalism and socialism? True, there have been transitional societies in the past. For centuries after the Renaissance individual capitals were growing within feudal society, gathering economic power, weakening the host, becoming more able and willing to seize political power. They could do so because the dynamic of capitalism – accumulation – does not and never did require centralized control over the whole of society in order to function. It is a dynamic that operates within autonomous units, small or large, and for that reason it could coexist with the localism, the traditionalism and subsistence-orientation of feudalism.

But socialism is a total system. It cannot grow piecemeal within the interstices of a capitalist society. How does workers' control of production coexist with control by a ruling class when the means of production in dispute are one and the same? How does self-determination and consumer sovereignty ('production for use') coexist with the external compulsion and blind accumulation that results from capitalist dispersal? There may be room for transitional forms in distribution, but at the level of production and control over production the only possible transition is a sudden, revolutionary one.

5.
The Politics of Confusion

It is useless to look for independent or critical thinking in Mandel. Nowhere in the two volumes is there a sense of fresh exploration or the feel that capitalism is posing old problems in new ways, and that the explanations need to be worked afresh out of the loose body of analysis written in the marxist tradition. On the contrary, doctrine is first, its use secondary: 'we seek to show', he announces in his Introduction, 'that it is possible, on

the basis of the scientific data of contemporary science, to recon-
stitute the whole economic system of Karl Marx'.[29] And in his
final chapter we find him still waving the truncheons of uncritical
orthodoxy: 'Marxism rejects . . . it readily admits . . . Marxism
explains'.[30]

Here at least Mandel is consistent. In the defence of
orthodoxy the medium becomes the message. Since facts are to
be paraded as so many defence witnesses rather than used to
explain what is actually happening, only the most docile, old
and used ones are selected. Since precision might entail a critical
inspection of the doctrine, it is drowned in irrelevant detail. And
since there are other Marxists who do better as critics of
the system, because they think rather than intone, they are
swept under the text into a footnote and their ideas passed
over.[31]

Vagueness and sloppiness swamp everything: parallel to
that bureaucracy which is only the *chief* [sic] director of accumulation' there is a working class whose 'conquest of power' and
whose 'socialization of the major means of production and exchange . . . fail of their purpose *to some extent* [sic] if they are
not accompanied by radical changes in the *atmosphere* [sic] in the
enterprise'.[32] Crude philosophical idealism suffuses every thought,
whether it is about the individual unconscious still harbouring
'echoes from the primitive communist past' of 7,000 years ago,
or about the amazing triumph of disembodied Marxist theory
'capable of inspiring, and not unsuccessfully, the economic
policy of states both large and small'.[33]

Behind it all lies a confusion between social power and its
packaging, between control and its forms. It is a congenial
confusion for Mandel because it allows him to practise his unique
fugitive accent – the easy shift from urban workers, to 'third
world' peasants, to students as the revolutionary focus; the rapid
transitions from reforms to 'structural reforms' to direct action as
the current tactic; the indiscriminate loving-up to the only

fixtures in his political world – the dissident and not so dissident bureaucracies of both Social-Democracy and Stalinism.

In the realm of theory it places him plumb in the centre of 'the school of "vulgar" economics – a school characterized by the abandonment of all attempts to systematize and synthesize'. [34]

1. Ernest Mandel, *Marxist Economic Theory*, translated from the French by Brian Pearce, London: Merlin Press 1968.

2. *ibid.*, p706 (emphasis in the original).

3. 'the totality of production . . . is urged onward only by the capitalists' thirst for profit. The private form of appropriation makes profit the only aim and driving force of production' (p171); 'Profit remains the purpose and driving force of capitalist production' (p561); and so on.

4. *ibid.*, pp568–9.

5. *ibid.*, p166.

6. *ibid.*

7. *ibid.*

8. *ibid.*, p167.

9. *ibid.*, pp529–34.

10. See pages 168, 171, 346, 437, 529 for a fair sample.

11. *ibid.*, p531.

12. *ibid.*, pp511, 520–1.

13. *ibid.*, pp488, 489.

14. Alfred Maizels, *Industrial Growth and World Trade*, Cambridge University Press 1963, p80.

15. Mandel, *op. cit.* pp436–7.

16. *ibid.*, p492.

17. *ibid.*, p.516.

18. *ibid.*, pp437, 437n.

19. *ibid.*, p574.

20. *ibid.*, p584.

21. *ibid.*, p631.

22. *ibid.*, p597.

23. *ibid.*, p561.

24. *ibid.*, p565 (emphasis in the original).

25. *ibid.*, p561.

26. *ibid.*, pp571–2.

27. *ibid.*, p564.

28. *ibid.*, pp572–3.

29. *ibid.*, p17.

30. *ibid.*, p726.

31. Three out of a 'number of sociologists [*sic!*] who try to make use of the Marxist method of analysis' are mentioned by name in a footnote to 'The Social Character of the Soviet Economy', a key section (p.560). The one whose ideas on the subject are most developed and who has succeeded in implanting them in an active, revolutionary organization – Tony Cliff – is not mentioned in the extensive bibliography nor referred to in the index. The one whose ideas are of an earlier vintage and less commanding, but who can still claim something of an organized following in Italy – Amedeo Bordiga – makes the index but not the bibliography. And the third – D.Dallin – with few, and reactionary, ideas and no following – makes both.

32. *ibid.*, p643.

33. *ibid.*, p13.

34. *ibid.*, p707.

Part Two

CENTRE AND PERIPHERY

5. Black Reformism: the Theory of Unequal Exchange

There are a number of explanations for the unending misery of the people in backward countries. One of them is the theory of unequal exchange which sees in international trade the mechanism for exploiting backward countries and in rising real wages in the West the trigger for that mechanism.[1]

I.

Unequal Exchange

Stripped to the bone, and expressed in the terms of its protagonists, the argument runs: if *all* factors of production in a competitive economy, not only capital and labour-power, but any direct or indirect component of production that can be used to enforce a claim to a share of the product, were fully mobile, each would receive a standard return wherever it was put to work; and the distribution of the product amongst the classes and groups which control the factors would be the same everywhere.

Where some factors are more mobile than others, the sharing of output amongst them will vary from place to place in accordance with the relative strength of the classes or groups in control of the less mobile factors. In these circumstances the mobile factor would not always and everywhere receive the standard expected return unless part of its total income shifted from where its share of product is relatively high to where it is relatively low. In other words, an uneven distribution of product within the system sets up flows of income from one part of it to another via the equalization of returns to the mobile factor or factors. Or, more starkly, the cost of any tax or rent imposed on the mobile factor anywhere in the system can be clawed back from the rest of it.

Where, as is the case today, the factors of production are not only unevenly mobile but are also confined in separate currency areas, with each currency area needing to balance its international payments over time, the only way of sustaining this flow is through unequal exchange in international trade, that is, trade in which the partners with relatively high primary returns to the mobile factors systematically price their products, or are forced to price their products, below value in terms of direct and indirect labour inputs, and those with relatively low primary returns to the mobile factor systematically charge more than value.

Since capital is now more mobile internationally than any other factor, more so than labour-power is or ever was, and very much more so, naturally, than land or government, the equalization of returns to the mobile factor is through the formation of a world average rate of profit.

The theory's protagonists see nothing new in this. Capital has always been mobile and so has always been vulnerable to squeezes from the relatively immobile factors of production. In eighteenth- and early nineteenth-century England, for example, the squeeze came from the landlords and their state in the form of high prices for protected food. What might have ended up as super-profits if capital were not mobile, or as a sustained decline in export prices if it were not squeezed, was converted into a super-rent retained in the country. The world was forced to pay so large a tribute to the English landlords that capital flowed perversely – *into* capital-rich England from the capital-hungry periphery.

Variations on the theme were played in pre-war Japan and post-revolutionary Russia where the state alone hampered the mobility of capital and so prevented the abnormally high primary profits that were being made from leaking abroad.

Today, the argument runs, the squeeze on capital is still going on, but the agent, in the developed West at least, is the working class. Since the 1860s [*sic*][2] or, more realistically, the 1880s when mass trade unionism emerged as a major social force, workers have pushed their real incomes far beyond physiological need. What Marx recognized as a 'historical and moral element' in wages has taken wing so that real wages in the West are now some thirty times the subsistence levels ruling in the backward countries of the South. Once again what might have ended up as super-profits for capital, or lower export prices to the rest of the world, is captured by an immobile factor, labour-power; the benefits of superior techniques are held in the countries in which they arise; and the backward countries are saddled with a constant, irreversible deterioration in their terms of trade to make good the loss of profits to capital in the North. It is they who are made to pay for the high and rising real wages of workers in the privileged heartlands and for the relative social harmony that has prevailed there. In the circumstances there can be no common working-class interest world-wide. The privileged workers in the North have a stake in high primary profits and in its corollary, low wages, in the South – as large a stake as they have in high wages and low primary profits at home. Naturally, the converse is true for the destitute workers in the South. For each group high profits (and low wages) are an advantage so long as they arise outside the range of its own mobility and so long as capital remains mobile.

At present only workers in the North benefit unequivocally from a free flow of profits. Workers in the South can wish

GCT

only to disrupt it, for it denies their countries the potential investment on which employment and, ultimately, wage rises hinge. 'The choice', writes Emmanuel in their name, 'is between unequal exchange and autarky'.

Unequal exchange is not new in marxist analysis: it is implicit in the stable coexistence of different branches of production with different internal structures (or organic compositions of capital) but similar rates of profit, and is covered therefore by the literature on the 'transformation problem'. Its application to the relations between the developed and backward regions of capitalism is also not new. Otto Bauer, Evgenyi Preobrazhenski, Henryk Grossman, Maurice Dobb and many others dealt with it in some form. What is new is the importance attached to the mechanism, the refinement with which it is presented and the political conclusions drawn from its existence.

2.

The Autonomy of Wages[3]

The contemporary theorists trace the course of North–South relations in the last hundred years or so to the rise in real wages in the capitalist centres. Wages are the 'independent variable of the system', its determinant.

In the North, the argument runs, wages are very much higher than they are in the South. Even after allowing for direct and indirect social benefits, for differences in the intensity of labour, for differences in the length of the labour year or in average skills, and for all other influences, there remains a large residue which simply cannot be explained in terms of the cost of maintaining labour-power. It is a super-wage, the product of wage-drive pure and simple, a Northern worker's luxury paid for by the entire population of the South, including its workers.

This distinction between the cost element and the luxury, or 'historic and moral', element of wages is crucial. The whole weight of contemporary writing on the subject rests on it. Yet astonishingly little has been done to justify it empirically. Emmanuel, for example, takes a broad factor of 30 as the difference between real wages in developed and backward countries and splits it evenly between the two elements: greater intensity of effort is awarded fifteen, and the 'historic and moral' element the other fifteen. That's it. The argument stops short where the arithmetic should begin.

For convenience and in order to present the unequal exchange argument in the most favourable light, Britain and India can be taken to represent the system's centre and its periphery respectively:

In 1966 net disposable income per wage-earning household, that is the amount actually available for maintaining and renewing the ability to work after taking into account taxes and subsidies and subsidiary earnings, was £1,100 in Britain[4] and Rs2006 in India.[5] This is not Emmanuel's 30 to 1 disparity, but it is still enormous – in the region of 7 to 1 at the official rate of exchange. However, since official rates of exchange obscure as much as they reveal, we shall ignore them.

The government recognized subsistence minimum in Britain in 1966 was £210·6 a year; in India it was Rs741.[6] The ratio of average income to subsistence income is therefore 1·93 times higher in Britain than in India. Taking as the unit of income the minimum required to keep a worker alive and working, the average British workers' household is paid almost twice as much as the average Indian worker's household.

If wages in the two countries were paid for equal abilities to work in terms of intensity and quality, that would be that. British workers would still be seen to be living in relative luxury – above the level required to maintain or renew that ability. Their wage would be higher than the cost of labour-power. In reality of course there are huge differences in the average worker's competence in the two countries. At any comparable level of skill the British worker is normally able to keep up an intensity and a consistency of effort far beyond anything his or her equivalent can do in India. Naturally there are exceptions to the rule.[7]

Also the rule is difficult to establish, but there is some evidence to suggest that under broadly similar conditions and with labour-power of similar skill, physical productivity in India is under a quarter of what it is in Britain.[8]

That means that the British : Indian wage ratio of 1·93 to 1 is *less* than the British : Indian productivity ratio of 4·44 to 1. In other words, *the cost of a unit of labour-power of similar quality is less in Britain than it is in India*. The cost of a unit of labour power in Britain is less than half – 43 per cent – of the cost in India.[9]

There is some sense in comparing groups of British and Indian workers of the same level of skill. There is none at all in comparing the average competence of all British and Indian workers at the same level of skill. For if there is one outstanding difference between the two it lies in the different degrees to which they are culturally enriched. The average British worker can be expected to read and drive; he or she will normally be able to handle a wide range of tools and concepts, and respond to a wide range of stimuli on the basis of knowledge rather than from personal experience. The Indian worker will not. The *average* competence of the two are obviously worlds apart qualitatively.

The cost of maintaining them effectively – their value – is bound to reflect this difference. For example, a truck driver dare not make a practice of sleeping at the wheel, and must therefore be able to ensure rest at home and a home to rest in; a bullock-cart driver dare and often does nod off, so his housing is less important to the employer (unless he uses the same roads as the truck driver!) and his wage will not need to contain as large a housing component. New entrants into a factory in Britain need to be able to read, and their parents' wages need to contain therefore a child-support and -education component. New mill hands in India need not, and usually do not, read, so the pressure on their parents' wages is less. And so on and on – there is no end to the comparisons that can be made.

These differences in the average competence required of workers in the centre of the capitalist system and at its periphery, and the related differences in the cost of their maintenance have grown with the ageing of the system and have had important effects. They explain, for example, why free international migration of workers has very nearly disappeared in the last fifty years despite an astounding growth in the world market for skilled labour and in its mobility between countries. For while it is true that the immediate reason for forming and reforming the apparatus of migration control has always been political or the outcome of some pressure-group activity, underlying their success is capital's balking at the prospect of having to pay the full wage and welfare cost of relatively skilled labour-power to workers who command – in its terms – an impaired competence.[10]

These differences explain also the unsteady but inexorable rise in worker's real incomes in Russia and Eastern Europe where the bureaucracy is being taught, sometimes spectacularly through mass revolt and the rolling of heads, always painfully, that the ability to work with skill cannot be maintained on a budget more or less adequate for reproducing crude labour-power.

Skills are costly to create and maintain, which is not to say that the workers who possess them do not *enjoy* the higher incomes they command. On the contrary: the car that might be necessary for the British worker to get to and from work – it is clearly necessary for the American one – incidentally provides services that are valued for themselves. High standards of health and education are enjoyable in spite of being necessary. In the circumstances, the fundamental distinction between cost and luxury can easily be blurred, particularly by writers from the peripheral countries of capitalism where the luxuries of the rich are often what workers in the centre use as necessities.

It is also true that real wage increases are not achieved without a fight; capital does not make a rational assessment of the maintenance costs for the constantly improving competence it requires from its workforce. For this reason wage increases or minimum wage laws can be, and are, dressed up by capital's propagandists as a forced entry into affluence, in the teeth of employer opposition. But that is only the appearance. The substance is that the system must adapt to the rising cost of maintaining an increasingly valuable average ability to work. It does so, as it does to most changes, blindly, unwillingly and through conflict. It needs better workers. Whether it likes it or not, it has to pay for them.

But how much does it pay? Having adjusted the average wage in Britain and India to take account of transfers and taxation, of productivity, and the cost of intensity of effort, can the same be done for the cost of maintaining different levels of average competence? It can't, at least not directly; but if the Indian and British armies can be said to represent, however crudely, the technological maturity of Indian and British capitalism (a comparison which favours India) and if the maintenance cost per enlisted man in these very similar institutions can be said to represent the basic cost of the average competence required in the two countries, we arrive at a skill premium for the average British worker of 476 at the official rate of exchange, or 121 at our own wages exchange rate.[11]

Taking the low figure and adjusting our previous results gives us a ratio of 0·63 : 1 for the cost to capital of a unit of average ability to work within the capitalist sector in Britain and India. What seems at first to be an enormous gap between British and Indian wages, and by extensions between wages in the centre and at the periphery of the capitalist system can be more than explained by the cost of maintaining the very different average abilities to work in the two countries. It has little to do with militancy, little to do with trade unionism, little to do with the 'institutional factors' which are supposed to have helped labour extract a rent from capital. *Workers in the North get more because they need more in order to produce much more better. In fact they are relatively underpaid in terms of the quantity and quality of their ability to work. They get much more per head than workers in the South, but they get much less per unit of labour-power. They are richer, but more exploited.*

3.

Centralization of Capital on a World Scale

The debate on wages separates the upholders of class and of national politics and is important for that reason. But from the point of view of the theory of unequal exchange it is irrelevant. Even if changes in real wages did affect profits and profit flows in the ways suggested, so would a change in the real return to any relatively immobile factor of production as defined by the unequal exchangeists – in taxes, for example, which have grown much faster than wages since the 1880s – per head of population, as a proportion of total product, or *in toto*, and this both West and East.

The crucial question for the theory as distinct from its politics is not what triggers the mechanism of unequal exchange but whether that mechanism exists at all, and if it does, how important it is. Let us start with relative importance.

The absolute scale of production is important for society. On it depend the type of technique that can be used and the range of articles that can be made. But for the individual capital absolute size as such is unimportant. It is simply an inevitable outcome of the drive for greater relative size. The single capital stands to gain in competition as much from a uniform reduction in the scale of its competitors' operations as from an unmatched increase in its own. So long as growth and destruction are allocated in its interests, it finds them equally welcome. Relative size is what counts.

This evenhanded attitude towards progress and retrogression on the part of the single capital is reflected in the mechanisms for centralizing capital. All of them naturally shift the relative scale of central and peripheral capital in the former's favour, but they range from the relatively benign to the malignant, from mechanisms that add (to A) but subtract not (from B) to those that add not (to A) but subtract a great deal (from B).

The oldest and least complicated is plain plunder – the 'primitive accumulation' of capital in the centre of the system through transferring the periphery's already-accumulated surpluses, in the form, usually, of precious metals and stones. In its pure form – as a tribute exacted from pre-capitalist societies – it is a net gain to capitalism, even if the gain accrues entirely to the centre. Clearly it is no loss to the as yet non-existent capitals in the South.

Pure 'primitive accumulation' or *positive centralization* was a limited device, bound by the smallness of pre-capitalist hoards and by the low productivity of the societies that created them. It gave way to a number of bastard varieties in which all or part of currently created surplus is transferred from the countries and capitals in which they arise to the centre. The tax tribute which sustained the colonies' export surpluses over a long period was one of these.

More typical of today is *neutral centralization* in which a transfer of surplus between capitals takes place, but with no net gain or loss to the system as a whole. The export of profits, fees and royalties, unless they are completely offset by 'aid' receipts, comes into this category. These amount to some $6 billion a year. Less well-known is the export of skilled manpower – the overt brain drain.

The mechanism is simple and brutal. Since the second world war the countries of the capitalist centre have refined their migration controls into highly selective instruments with which to compete for skilled migrants while rejecting unskilled labour-power. The result now is that a significant proportion of graduates in the South is sucked into the advanced countries particularly in technical and scientific fields. There are no overall figures but some idea of the extent of drain can be gained from the fact that three countries only – France, Canada and the US – absorbed more than half the engineers graduating in Iran and Syria, and a third of such graduates in Chile and the Lebanon between 1962 and 1966. More than five times Hong Kong's total output of engineering graduates in these years migrated to the same three countries. The same goes for natural scientists: three-fifths of Hong Kong's graduates, half of Venezuela's, a fifth of Chile's and the Philippines' travelled the same route in the same period; as did two-thirds of Hong Kong's new physicians, one quarter of Lebanon's or Chile's and one-fifth of the Philippines'.[12]

The cost of this explicit brain drain to the emigrant countries is immeasurable. One partial estimate puts the direct cost of educating the migrant graduates at some half billion dollars at today's prices.[13] This sum does not include the costs of maintaining them during their student life. It does not reflect the damage caused the drained society through losing a young labour force, the members of which it can be supposed, are the brightest, most inventive and most energetic of their class and age;[14] or the damage caused that society by restricting its capacity to absorb scientific advances made elsewhere. It does not measure the cost of creating the manual skills that drain away in larger absolute numbers – the 600,000 carpenters, mechanics, repairmen, nurses and so on that migrate yearly.[15] This alone might cost over $\frac{1}{4}$ billion in direct outlay every year.[16]

Above all it does not begin to touch on the cost of distorting the whole structure of education in the South – the curricula, the models, the criteria of excellence – which makes the migration of skills possible,[17] and which contributes to the incredibly high dropout rates at every step up the education ladder in the South. If we assume Latin American rates to apply to the South as a whole and the cost of schooling and college education in five backward countries studied by the United Nations Institute for Training and Research to be equally representative, the direct cost of educational wastage in the South must be of the order of $13 billion a year.[18] That means that the *direct costs* of educating the migrants and of the waste associated with maintaining an educational system compatible with the needs of the capitalist centres can be no less than $14 billion a year, and might be several times more.[19]

Similar in effect although even less open to scrutiny is the *covert* brain drain in the South – the absorption of skills locally by foreign-controlled or 'multinational' companies. Here too the best products of the local educational establishment are absorbed by foreign capital; a proportion of educational and other social capital is annexed in everything but name by the foreign firms; and curricula are distorted to serve the employment needs of the biggest and best employers – the foreign companies – and of their local imitators.

This covert brain drain is an aspect of a larger mechanism, equally neutral, for centralizing capital – the direct transfer of control over local surplus to foreign capital *in situ*, without any physical displacement. The multinational firm abroad usually controls a far larger range and quantity of assets than it owns in any legal sense. Most of its finance – sometimes more than half of its share capital, and very often the vast bulk of its loan capital – is subscribed locally, and derives from locally-produced surplus.

Its labour is local; its management is mostly so and its technical cadres almost entirely so. It is also able to command a proportion of the host country's social capital and government services in the same way as it absorbs part of the country's privately appropriated surplus – in a real sense, that proportion is annexed.

It is difficult to put a figure on foreign-control-without-ownership. But if India is still doing duty as an example, and if the relative position of foreign capital in the country has not changed substantially in the past decade, the ratio of foreign-controlled to foreign-owned capital in the private sector is something like 2·4 : 1 and its share of the surplus appropriated by that sector about two fifths.[20] Assuming further that the foreign-controlled sector absorbs a similar proportion of government current account expenditure, something like 12 per cent of the Indian surplus outside of agriculture is annexed by foreign capital.[21]

Multiplied worldwide[22] and making every allowance for the crudity of the arithmetic and the recklessness of its implicit assumptions, Northern capital in the South was absorbing some $5\frac{1}{4}$ billion a year in the mid-sixties, or $10 billion at current prices – as direct a transfer of surplus as any, notwithstanding the fact that most of it remained physically where it was.

An even more subtle and obscure form of centralization takes place via the arms trade. What appears to be normal international trade, or even the exchange of equivalents, in which a handful of countries at the centre exchange their typical products for the typical products of a large number of countries at the periphery, is in fact an exchange of *necessarily* unproductive resources for potentially productive ones, or the exchange of 'dead' surplus for 'live' surplus. To be more specific, the tea that India sells Russia in exchange for MiGs, or the coffee Brazil supplies in exchange for US missiles and anti-guerilla training, or the oil Britain gets from the Persian Gulf in exchange for whole armouries, is consumed by Russian, or American or British workers, and is productive, in principle at least, for that reason.

But the tea- or coffee- or oil-equivalent received by India or Brazil or the Persian Gulf States in the form of weapons or weapon instruction is not consumed by workers and can never be. It can never enter the productive process in those countries, however indirectly. It is utterly sterile.[23] What the exchange has done is shift potentially productive surplus from India to Russia, or from Brazil to the United States, or the Middle East to Britain and waste in the opposite direction. From the point of view of the capitals involved, *it is a one-way transfer of investible surplus which takes place even on the assumption of equal exchange.* Worldwide this transfer accounts for some $5·8 billion a year.[24]

So far we have kept within the bounds of benign centralization in which the relative sizes of capitals change in consequence of shifts of surplus into the system (positive centralization) or in consequence of shifts between individual capitals within it (neutral centralization). The size of the system either grows or remains the same. We now need to look at the alarming and increasingly pertinent case of *negative* centralization in which changes in the relative sizes of individual capitals lead directly to a decline in the size of the total system – a form of retrogressive transfer through surplus destruction. War is an extreme example. But there are a million and one ways short of war in which weaker capitals can be made to dissipate their surpluses rather than use them. If for example they buy modern arms, they must also buy a package of local expenditures to make them work, and so end up sterilizing more of their realized surplus.[25] If they buy modern plant, they must buy an associated package of local overheads and of administrative and sales devices that absorbs still more, not always productively.

They are compelled to make huge, single-shot expenditures in facilities for which the minimum sizes are set by the immense capitals of the North in terms of their own huge absolute sizes, gained after decades of concentrating the world's surpluses in their hands. The minima have now become so large that no country in the South can hope to attain them on its own. None can hope to bring together what it takes to exchange equal values with the advanced capitals or to exchange equal clout.

There is a mountain of evidence. Backward countries are strewn with broken-backed prestige projects and prestige industries – witnesses to the occasions when the effort was made but failed for lack of scale. Banks in the financial centres are cluttered with offshore accounts, product of a 'perverse' flow of capital from the South, and witnesses to the occasions, more numerous, when the effort was not even made. The evidence covers conspicuous middle-class consumption in the South, the uncontrolled expansion of their bureaucracies;[26] the growing absolute number of their illiterates and ex-literates;[27] and many of the structural distortions 'blocking' capitalist development.

What the evidence means in terms of pounds and pence is harder to say. However, if there is any reality in the text-book figures and quantitative relationships normally adduced for backward countries, and if it is right to believe that the high and rising threshold sizes for participation in the capitalist system are beyond the reach of all backward countries without exception,[28] the loss to the system in the form of surplus generated but wasted must be in the region of $65 billion a year at 1972 prices: total surplus currently available to government and business (at 20 per cent of total gross domestic product in the South or $77 billion at 1972 prices plus net transfers on public 'aid' account of about $5 billion) less the absolute transfers already mentioned. This sum is a crude measure of relative centralization.

Compare these figures – speculative as they are – with those given by the protagonists of the theory as the loss to the South from unequal exchange. Amin reaches a total for unrequited transfer of $22 billion a year, $8 billion of which is in the modern sector and the rest in the traditional sector.[29] Our own total is $82 billion: $0·75 billion for actual brain drain; $10 billion for the direct attachment of surplus *in situ*; $5·8 billion for the exchange of productive for sterile surplus; $65 billion for the waste due to the non-clearance by the South of the high threshold sizes imposed by the North. Even if we ignore the downward bias of these estimates, and the non-inclusion of many other forms of benign centralization – the exchange of non-military waste for productive surplus, the migration of unskilled labour, the absorption of surplus in the South by Northern state capital – it is clear that unequal exchange *as measured by the theory's protagonists* is not the characteristic instrument of centralization in the current period, nor even the 'elementary transfer mechanism . . . that . . . enables the advanced countries to begin and regularly to give new impetus to that *unevenness of development* that sets in motion all the other mechanisms of exploitation and fully explains the way that wealth is distributed'.[30]

Given the size and scope of the transfers that are taking place, it requires a very academic understanding of the terms to agree that 'if a country's trade balance, visible and invisible, is neutral or negative, this country can be exploited by its trading partners only if unit prices are implicated'. Whoever believes that, and the ensuing corollary that 'everything else is merely the paperwork of bankers and the verbal acrobatics of economists'[31] is blind to the variety of exploitation of the South by big Northern capital, and is condoning it by default.

4.

The Immobility of Capital

The argument for unequal exchange is usually couched in terms of advanced country A trading with backward country B, two independent and competing authorities of unequal strength, and with capital flowing between them. Although this type of formulation is hallowed in academic tradition, and although it is of some relevance to current trade between the state-capitalist countries and, temporarily and very partially, to trade between some of the others in war-time, it has little relevance to international commerce as it actually takes place, particularly between the North and the South. Such trade is not between *countries* A and B, but between *capitals* A and B, or parts of the same capitals in *both* A and B.[32] These capitals are essentially immobile.

Nothing need be said about the immobility of state capital. It is that by definition. But what about private capital – the sixty or so billion dollars worth ($85 billion at market value) of direct investments in the South? How mobile is it in practice?

The typical foreign investment today forms part of a very large 'multinational' corporation with headquarters in the North: 187 of the largest US corporations own four fifths of all US assets abroad;[33] much the same is true of European and Japanese investments. It is true of the investments whatever they happen to be in: oil and metal mining, industry proper and even plantations – the units of capital are immense, 'multinational' and the decisions directly affecting them are taken in New York, London, Tokyo or Paris.

This was not always the case. Sixty or seventy years ago although there were similarly large international companies operating in the colonies, the *typical* foreign investment was smaller, regionally-directed by expatriates or settlers, Anglo-thises or Franco-thats – large in local terms certainly, but not so large or so independent of local resources as to be able to dispense with a protective colonial state; dependent on its metropolitan links but not so deeply as is the typical local affiliate on its parent or headquarter company today.

It is not that the parent supplies indispensible fixed capital assets or finance – that happens and is important, but local capital and loans are usually to be had for the asking, at least in the larger countries of the South. Nor does the parent company necessarily provide exceptionally skilled technicians or managers – although it often does so and in some location-tied industries like oil this service is indispensable; in most other cases most of the higher staff are recruited locally. The parent is also not always essential for the original or ongoing supply of technology, although it often is, since local scientific resources cannot always satisfy the demands made by modern industry. In most cases, however, the foreign investors' operations in the South are routine, and whatever technological and scientific sophistication it requires is usually built into the machinery and procedures brought from abroad rather than added in process. In effect, there is no one area or function in which the parent company is always indispensible to its subsidiaries or affiliates in the South and therefore no single controlling device open to it. It is simply that the size and spread of the typical internationally-investing corporation is so immense that it can almost always supply the scarce factor whatever it happens to be at any time: finance, techniques, skills, materials, components and so on. In other words, what the large multinational corporation actually provides is, above all, insurance – a guarantee against uncertainty and unwelcome change. That is what permits its local affiliates to specialize farther and to grow faster than its purely local rivals dare.

In effect foreign firms in the South might look auto-nomous; they are often huge in their own right; *but they are only part of a larger irreducible unit.* If the local affiliate appears particularly profitable, that is because it belongs to the larger unit. If it seems particularly mobile, either in the crude geo-graphic sense implied but not explored in the theory of unequal exchange, or in the sense used here, of being able to encroach at will on locally-generated surpluses, it is because of the support given by belonging to that larger unit. And since the larger irreducible unit owes its size to the size of the economy in which it is based, it is more or less permanently anchored.

One can go further to say that the basic unit of capital in effect, if not in law and not in analysis or ideology, is larger than even the largest individual company; that the scope of the technical division of labour, or planning, of which it is part, as distinct from that of the social division of labour or the market, embraces the 'economy' or 'country' or 'state' or even, fitfully and weakly, a group of states like the EEC and its periphery. In these terms, some capitals like the American or to a less extent the Japanese are larger than their 'national capitals' by the addition of their 'multinational' corporations; others are more or less as large as their national capitals, like the Russian for example or – one suspects – the British where national and non-national multinationals probably cancel out one another; and some capitals are smaller, sometimes very much smaller, as in the South where the multinationals are exclusively part of one or other foreign capital.

Whatever their size all capitals are now so irreducibly huge and so embedded in national political structures they simply cannot be mobile in any real sense. A theory that rests on the assumption of mobility is built on sand.

Not that unequal exchange is unreal. It is, like the colonial tax tribute, one of the bastard forms of primitive accumulation or positive centralization. It reached a peak of importance for western capitalism during the colonial era and, for eastern state capitalism, during the Stalinist era. It still exists on the margins of the system in the backward South where dwarf capitals exact what they can in tax and other forms from the non-capitalist societies they occupy. But as between immobile independent capitals competing and compounding in world markets without the use of force it does not and cannot exist.

5.

The Politics of Unequal Exchange

The academic manifestation of unequal exchange is disconcerting. An abstruse and extended critique of Ricardo is

HCT

used to call bourgeois economics to account for its unreality; Marx is made to fight on an issue that could not have interested him – the workings of an *incomplete* capitalism. The theory itself is tied tightly to the behaviour of wages in the West, yet need not be. It is made dependent on the mobility of capital, yet on the evidence of its protagonists' own writings, surplus is what moves rather than capital. It is presented as the only mechanism for the transfer of that surplus, yet it is clearly one of many. Somehow one thing does not lead to another in the standard expositions except by way of erudite non-sequitur.

Intellectual disarray on this scale provokes probing, and since the theory's exponents are not fools, they must be judged to be naives, politically-motivated.

They start off soundly enough by rooting economic backwardness in economic drain: the dominated countries are plundered of the surplus that otherwise would have gone into extending their productive apparatus. The theorists do not deny other mechanisms at work – they recognize the self-reinforcing attraction of capital towards the largest markets, the similar self-reinforcing specialization of the South in low-skill labour-intensive occupations, and so on. They even derive these directly from 'the disparity between wage levels that produces unequal exchange' and so 'independently of this draining off process', but there is no doubt in their minds that these other 'blocking' mechanisms play subordinate parts.

And they are right. But then, having fixed on drain as the cause of backwardness, they leap onto its opposite as the answer to development. All that is needed for the backward countries to break into successful capitalist growth is to trap the outflow or to reverse its direction: slap a tax on exports, proposes Emmanuel. Go for autarky and diversification. Use the North's own weapon against it by forcing through high wages in the South – that might induce not merely a flow of surplus in the right direction, but even a flow of capital.

How these proposals are expected to materialize or which are to be preferred are never made clear. Nor does it matter, since in principle all of them can be implemented. For so long as capital is mobile and so long as this mobility is achieved through the mechanism of unequal exchange which – to repeat – is an *'accidental feature'* of capitalism, *not a structural necessity*,[34] the direction of the flow depends on bargaining and on nothing else.

The assumption of mobility is clearly not just an aid to analysis. It is a programmatic implement. It rests on a prior assumption of some power – that capital is infinitely divisible. If that is true there can be no threshold sizes for investment at any time; no irreducible size of productive capital below which it would not be able to exchange equal values with other existing capitals.

In a more general sense, if the premise of infinite divisibility were well-founded, capital would always and only be essence, never appearance; always a principle, never an institution historically determined. Politically, if capital were infinitely divisible, development and growth would always be possible within the system no matter how narrow their starting base. Capitalism could still expand. Hundreds of millions of people for whom even the most savage exploitation is better than the torment of literal redundancy could still choose to join it. All that would be needed is to adjust capitalism somehow, to tame it.

This is the reformist marrow of the theory. It is a black, 'third-world' and gutsy-sounding variety, but a reformism nonetheless. Like all reformisms it looks to capital to temper the system's worst effects. For that reason it dare not confront the system, not even intellectually through close inspection. So like all modern reformism it is still bewildered by state-capitalism: Russia is a country – we are told – which is socialist internally but capitalist in its relations with the outside world;[35] a country which long ago opted for the socialist path of development whose hallmark, naturally, is low wages and massive accumulation, in preference to the notorious capitalist path of high wages and massive centralization.[36]

Like all reformism it finds no difficulty in substituting labour for capital as the enemy in practice: cutting Northern workers down to Southern size will do just as well as shovelling Southern profits into Southern wage packets. And, like all reformisms it is crippled by its lack of a sense of history.

6.
Conclusion

So long as individual capitals were too small in aggregate to absorb the surplus available for productive investment, capital was mobile: it could migrate, it could form spontaneously on the margins of the capitalist centres of the time. The system could extend. Once the threshold size for an individual capital rose above that limit in aggregate, that is once the surplus could not sustain both the (faster) growth of existing capitals and the formation of (larger) new ones, immobility set in. The extension of the system in the strict sense of capital replication, or in a looser sense of proletarianizing a growing proportion of the world's population, ended. As the system aged further and individual capitals grew larger, the surplus available became inadequate to sustain all existing capitals. Some had to go and, in the process, a new critical minimum expenditure, on arms and therefore unproductive this time but equally compelling, was claimed of the social surplus, further crippling its ability to sustain the system. At this stage the system contracts in the strict sense that the number of capitals lessens, or more loosely, that the world undergoes relative deproletarianization.

This is not the place to deal with the extension and contraction of the system in any detail. It is enough to say that the number of productive industrial workers as a proportion of the active labour force in the world as a whole has fallen since World War II. Even in the capitalist heartlands, despite an unprecedented and almost unbelievable growth of some 68 million in the industrial labour force,[37] more and more people are being excluded from production, unable to cope with the increasing pace and skill demanded of workers by the mighty tension-ridden capitals that employ them: the prematurely aged, the dropout and many of the apparent social, psychological and physical invalids. Even here, despite an unprecedented flow of prime labour-power from the edges of the system, the number of wage earners as a proportion of population has been declining, even if only slightly.[38]

The capitalist system is becoming smaller in relation to society. The working class is becoming smaller in relation to humanity at large. A few grotesque concentrations of economic and social power blot out the future for most people on earth. What is needed now is an analysis of stagnation, not a theory of expansion; revolution not anachronistic attempts at reform.

1. During the 1960s the discussion of unequal exchange was restricted more or less to readers of French, and particularly to readers of *Cahiers de l'ISEA* and *Problèmes de Planification*. The arguments are now becoming accessible in English. The most elaborate exposition is in Arghiri Emmanuel, *Unequal Exchange. A study of the imperialism of trade*, London: New Left Books 1972. In addition there are Emmanuel, 'White-Settler Colonialism and the Myth of Investment Imperialism', *New Left Review* 73, May–June 1972; Christian Palloix, 'The Question of Unequal Exchange: A Critique of Political Economy', *Bulletin of the Conference of Socialist Economists* 2, 1 Spring 1972; Geoff Pilling, 'Political Economy and Imperialism: the Work of Arghiri Emmanuel', *Economy and Society*, Vol. 2, no.2, May 1973; and a number of less accessible articles in journals as far away as, for example, the *New Zealand Left*

Books Review, or the *Review of Radical Political Economics* in the US.

2. Emmanuel, *Unequal Exchange,* p49.

3. I am grateful to Amartya Sen for pointing out inconsistencies in an earlier draft of this section.

4. Average gross household wage-income in 1966 was £1,432, of which 77 per cent was left for free disposal. (From Central Statistical Office, *Annual Abstract of Statistics 1972,* London: HMSO 1972, Table 79, p78; and 'The Incidence of Taxes and Social Security Benefits, particularly among households with low incomes', *Economic Trends,* July 1968, Tables I iii–vi, ppxxxiii–xxxvi.)

5. This is a weighted average wage for 'registered' workers in the industries listed in the table below less estimated indirect taxes plus estimated subsidies and excluding secondary earnings contributed by women and children.

Wages:

India: *Registered employment and average annual earnings, per head 1966*

Sector	Employment (m)	Earnings (Rs)
Plantations	1·13	764
Mining/quarrying	0·67	1581
Manufacturing	4·53	2114
Utilities	0·31	2280
Transport/communications	2·21	2047
Weighted annual average income		1890

Sources: Government of India, *Economic Survey 1970–1971,* Delhi, 1971, Tables 3.1, 3.2, pp109–10; Tea Board of India, *Tea Statistics 1969–1970,* Calcutta: Tea Board 1970, Tables 26c, 27, pp111–28; The Statistical Section, Coffee Board, *Coffee Statistics 1968–1969,* Bangalore: The Secretary, Coffee Board 1970, Table XVII, pp287–302; Labour Bureau, Ministry of Labour and Employment, *Indian Labour Statistics 1971,* Simla, 1971, Tables 2.3, 4.1, 4.2, pp37, 55, 57; *Indian Labour Yearbook 1966,* Simla, 1968, Table 2.19, p61, and *1968,* Simla 1970, Table 2.18, p67.

The final figure Rs1890 is probably a fair approximation to an average urban wage for that year, since the downward bias imparted by the relatively low-paid plantation and mining workers (13 and 8 per cent of the total respectively) is offset by the exclusion of similarly low-paid 'unregistered' (small-industry) urban workers. The figure is understated to the extent of women's and children's contribution to total household wage income, which is still fairly important in urban India (although clearly less than in a rural setting).

Taxes:

It is assumed that Indian workers pay no direct taxes and that the incidence of all indirect taxes other than that on motor spirit is pro portional to income. Assuming further that agricultural labour income averaged Rs660 in 1966 (from *Indian Labour Statistics 1971*, Table 4.9, p63) total indirect tax revenue for 1966 divided by total population weighted by income gives Rs35 for indirect taxation per working-class household.

Benefits:

The money value of benefits and employers' contributions in manufacturing (including gas and electricity distribution) was Rs230 per employee per year. (Government of India, Central Statistical Organization, *Annual Survey of Industries, 1965*, Calcutta (nd) Vol. 1, p4.)

Assuming the same ratio of benefits to wages in the sectors listed above, but that employees' contributions (to state pension schemes, etc.,) do not exist outside manufacturing and utilities, average gross benefits were Rs151 per head.

6. In Britain, the rate of supplementary benefit for a single householder 'directly responsible for rent' in 1966 was £4·05 per week. (Central Statistical Office, *Social Trends in 1971*, London: HMSO 1971, Table 42, p88.)

This is a subsistence allowance based on physiological needs and excluding so far as possible, the 'historic and moral element' in wages. The official estimation of these needs has not changed in essentials since the 1890s or before (see A.B. Atkinson, 'Who are the Poorest?' *New Society*, 1 March 1973, pp466–8).

In India, minimum cost urban subsistence diet approved by the National Nutritional Advisory Committee and confirmed by Dr Kalyan Bagchi, Nutritional Adviser to the Ministry of Health was estimated at Rs1·49 per adult 'equivalent consumption unit' per day in Bombay (Rs1·4 in Bangalore) in 1968 (*Indian Labour Journal*, December 1968, pp1650–1) or Rs1·32 per day in 1966 prices.

The minimum clothing requirement per urban adult was estimated by the Committee of the Indian Labour Conference in 1962 to be 18 yards of cotton textile a year, or Rs40·35 in 1966 prices.

The minimum rent charged by the Government for an open

developed plot in Bombay or Calcutta – Rs6·50 per month in 1960 – is taken as basic for housing costs; and fuel, light, etc., is assumed to form a fifth of total subsistence expenditure, in line with official estimates (Government of India, Ministry of Labour and Employment, *Tripartite Conclusions 1942–1962*, Delhi, 1962, p49). On these assumptions, a weekly subsistence budget per adult male in urban India was Rs14·25 in 1966.

7. For some examples see Michael Kidron, *Foreign Investments in India*, London: Oxford University Press 1965, p249.

8. J.M.Healey ('Industrialization, Capital Intensity and Efficiency', *Oxford Institute of Economics and Statistics Bulletin*, November 1968, Table 1 p327) concludes that the productivity of operatives in India relative to the UK in the most 'capital intensive' that is, machine-paced or continuous-process industries, is 44·71 per cent and that it declines sharply the lower the level of fixed investment per head, to a low of 14·21 per cent. The weighted average is 22·50 per cent.

9. An incidental result of these comparisons is the emergence of an exchange rate which reflects the purchasing power of the wage packet more closely than the official rate. This wages-purchasing-power parity rate based on subsistence is Rs3·5 to the Pound at 1966 prices. This exchange rate has not been used in calculating relative exploitation. It is a result implicit in the calculations.

10. The full costs are not always paid of course. At the time of writing the EEC foreign ministers were resisting pressure to concede full welfare rights to migrant labour from the Maghreb countries since doing so 'would give workers from these countries privileged treatment over those from Turkey or Yugoslavia' (*Guardian* 5 June 1973). Throughout western capitalism, there are pockets of bonded-labour systems for migrants which effectively deny the workers trapped in them the normal social and legal protection. But the social, political and administrative costs of special treatment for migrants as an underclass are heavy and unacceptable in the long run to large-scale bureaucratically-organized capital.

11. Average annual outlay on pay, allowances, maintenance, etc per enlisted man in the army, that is, excluding procurement, equipment maintenance and so on, was: in India – Rs3094·8; in Britain – £1103·8 in the five years 1965/66 – 1969/70 (figures from the United Kingdom, *Defence Estimates (Army)*, relevant years; Government of India, *Defence Service Estimates*, relevant years). See note 9 for the wage-exchange rate.

12. S.Watanabe, 'The Brain Drain from Developing to Developed Countries', *International Labour Review*, April 1969, Table v, pp414–15.

13. G.Henderson, 'Emigration of Highly Skilled Manpower from the Developing Countries', UNITAR research Report no.3, 1970, p119.

14. Henderson *op. cit.*, p118 gives an estimate of $2 billion on account of this loss.

15. Watanabe, *op. cit.*, Table 1, pp404–5; Henderson, *loc.cit.*

16. Assuming such people to have had a secondary education and for that to have cost a total of $429 in direct government outlay at primary and secondary levels (unweighted average for five countries, 1968–69, taken from *The Brain Drain from Five Developing Countries*, UNITAR Research Report no.5, 1971, Table 7, p148).

17. Cf. the verbal testimony submitted by Dr Charles Sprague, Dean, Southwestern Medical School, University of Texas, to the US House of Representatives, Committee on Government Operations, Research and Technical Programs Subcommittee: 'In the Philippines, for example, there are proprietary institutions which, seemingly, have as a major objective the preparation of physicians to come to the United States for graduate education and hopefully to pursue professional practice of medicine in this country.' (*Hearings on The Brain Drain of Scientists, Engineers and Physicians from the Developing Countries to the US*, 90th Congress, Second Session, 23 January, 1968, p63.)

18. Dropout rates from William C. Thiesenhusen's written testimony, *ibid.* pp28–30; average cost per head in Cameroon, Colombia, Lebanon, Philippines, Trinidad and Tobago from *The Brain Drain from Five Developing Countries*, UNITAR Research Report no.5, 1971, Table 7, p148; enrolment figures from UNESCO, *Statistical Yearbook* 1971, Table 2.2.

19. The Reuss Committee quoted in footnote 17 concluded: 'If the cost of education and training received by emigrants is assessed in terms of the basic education and literacy foregone by their countries in having higher education systems, the loss of scientific professionals to developing countries is clearly very high, though not calculable in dollars-and-cents terms.' (*Report on the Brain Drain*, etc., p5.)

20. Kidron, *op. cit.*, p186.

21. Two-fifths of private investment *in industry* (from Government of India, Planning Commission, *Fourth Five Year Plan, a draft outline*, New Delhi, 1966, Table 7, p11), plus two-fifths

of public outlay on *administration* (Government of India, Central Statistical Office, *Brochure on Revised Series of National Product for 1960–61 to 1964–65*, New Delhi, (?) 1967, cited in R.K.Hazari, 'The Public Sector in India', in E.A.G.Robinson and Michael Kidron (eds), *Economic Development in South Asia*, London: Macmillan, p93), came to Rs577 crores in the mid-sixties. Assuming the usable surplus outside agriculture (taxes and domestic savings) to be 23 per cent of gross domestic product (from the above two sources) or Rs4,984 crores, the share of foreign capital in this part of the surplus is 11·6 per cent.

22. India's share of the South's gross domestic product is given as $41·5 billion out of a total $281·8 billion in 1967 (from United Nations, *World Economic Survey 1969–70*, New York: United Nations 1971, Table A 1, pp177–9).

23. See Chapter 2 above.

24. Value of major weapons exports to the South in 1971 at 1968 prices – $1·8 billion (Stockholm International Peace Research Institute, *World Armaments and Disarmament 1972*, Table 5A.1, pp120–1) doubled to $3·6 billion at 1968 prices to give total arms exports (from SIPRI, *The Arms Trade with the Third World*, Stockholm: Almqvist and Wiksell 1971, p83); and adjusted for price increases for arms of 10 per cent per year (as given in SIPRI, *World, etc, loc. cit*). to give $5·8 billion in 1973 at current prices). These monetary values are approximate and extremely conservative (see *ibid* pp4–7 for the extent to which arms imports into the South are under-recorded and underestimated). They are also net of military aid.

Military aid is not part of the centralizing process, at least not directly. It merely shifts waste about. Nor, in principle, are non-military loans and grants. Even the part of economic 'aid' which is spent on balance-of-payments support and which for that reason can be said to sustain the continued flow of profits, royalties, fees, interest and other payments from South to North does not come into it.

Such aid does induce centralization of capital, but indirectly. The effect is felt within the North, rather than between South and North, for the 'aid' is paid out of taxes levied regressively on small and medium-sized businesses at the centre, while the profits and other payments whose repatriation it sustains accrue by and large to the biggest of its capitals. The South participates in this case as a conduit, not as a victim.

In practice 'economic aid' can be and often is a method of dumping non-arms waste in the South, at a price; in practice it need not and often does not cover all the foreign-exchange costs of foreign investments, while yet covering enough to keep the payments going; and it often lubricates one or other form of unequal exchange. But in principle it is not one of the mechanisms for centralizing capital internationally.

25. SIPRI reports that repair and maintenance costs of major weapons and the cost of establishing and maintaining adequate repair shops and the various support services for effective field organization come to 'several times' the initial price *in a developed country*; and that they are very much higher 'in a developing country with a low level of technical education' (*Arms Trade*, p84).

26. Excluding the armed forces, India has over 10 million Central and State Government employees compared with 3 million twenty years ago (Prem Shankar Jha, *The Guardian*, 23 May 1973). The armed forces have grown in roughly the same proportion – from under 300,000 to 960,000.

27. In 1968, 924 million people or 42 per cent of the world's population over 15 years old – were thought to be illiterate. The number was growing – by 40 million between 1950 and 1960 (Thiesenhusen, *loc. cit.*, p27).

28. The case is argued in Chapter 9, below.

29. Samir Amin, *L'accumulation à l'échelle mondiale*, Paris: Editions Anthropos 1971, pp75, 76.

30. Emmanuel, *op. cit.*, p265 (emphasis in original).

31. Emmanuel, p367.

32. Paradoxically, the unequal exchangists model is truer to life as it was at the beginning of the 'era of unequal exchange', when the colonial state often held the balance between home-based and colony-based metropolitan capital, each acting independently in world trade, than it is today. Now, most North–South trade can be assumed to take place either between governments or between the components of large international companies.

33. Raymond Vernon, *Sovereignty at Bay*, New York and London: Basic Books 1971, p18.

34. Emmanuel, *op. cit.*, pp163, 169, 330–1 *passim*.

35. Amin, *op. cit.*, p12.

36. Emmanuel, *op. cit.*, pp133, 379.

37. ILO, *Yearbook of Labour Statistics 1970*, p11.

38. *ibid.*

6. Imperialism: Highest Stage but One

Fate was unkind to Lenin when it singled out his pamphlet, *Imperialism, The Highest Stage of Capitalism*, to be the most pervasive of his writings. The warning implied in its subtitle – 'A Popular Outline' – and made explicit in the original preface – 'these cramped passages . . . crushed . . . in an iron vice, distorted on account of the censor'; the narrowly-conceived objective 'to present . . . *a general picture* of the world capitalist system in its international relationship *at the beginning of the twentieth century* . . .';[1] the fact that the pamphlet was purpose-written to explain the causes of World War I, then at its height – have all been lost sight of in an uncritical, almost universal, acceptance of its central themes. This is all the more strange since much of what he analysed has clearly either gone or become much less important than in his day.

In broadest outline, Lenin's thesis was that capitalism's maturity compels it to export capital on a large scale and that its internal organization facilitated the process. The drive to export capital resulted in a carve-up of the world financially between cartels and territorially between empires, and the profits accruing therefrom provided the wherewithal to bribe a thin upper-crust of workers into acquiescence with reformism at home and with imperialism abroad.

First published in *International Socialism* 9, Summer 1962.

There are at least four issues here. First, how relevant is Lenin's portrait of capitalism today? Second, is reformism necessarily tied to empire? Third – a problem which moved from the wings only after the decline of classic marxism – how has the flow and ebb of imperialism affected the development of backward countries and of the socialist movement within them? And fourth, does all this modify our view of internationalism? Since these are fundamental issues which require detailed treatment, I shall deal with only one, the first, here, leaving the others for later issues of *International Socialism*.

1.
Monopoly

Lenin starts with the advanced stage of capitalist concentration in the industrial countries. 'The transformation of competition into monopoly,' he writes, 'is one of the most important – if not the most important – phenomena of modern capitalist economy . . .' (p15).

It was and still is. And since his day the process has gone on at an increasing rate. In post-war Britain, for example, expenditure on successful takeovers of firms big enough to be quoted on the stock exchange has risen from an average of £40 million a year between 1949 and 1952, to about £100 million yearly between 1953 and 1957 and up to £300 million yearly in 1959 and 1960. By then takeovers were more frequent than company flotations so that the number of 'quoted' companies fell by about 100 in each of the last two years.[2] Since 1962 the prospect of Britain joining the Common Market must have increased the number of mergers even more, in line with what has occurred on the Continent.[3] And, as concentration had already gone a long way before this post-war spurt,[4] it must have reached phenomenal proportions by now.

2.
'Finance Capital'

Lenin goes on to show that concentration in industry was paralleled by a similar movement in banking to such effect that the banks in practice gained control of commerce and industry. In extenso: 'When carrying the current accounts of a few capitalists, the banks, as it were, transact a purely technical and exclusively auxiliary operation. When, however, these operations grow to enormous dimensions we find that a handful of monopolists control all the operations, both commercial and industrial, of capitalist society. They can, by means of their banking connexions, by running current accounts and transacting other financial operations, first *ascertain exactly* the position of the various capitalists, then *control* them, influence them by restricting or enlarging, facilitating or hindering their credits, and finally they can *entirely determine* their fate, determine their income, deprive them of capital, or, on the other hand, permit them to increase their capital rapidly and to enormous proportions, etc.' (p31, emphasis in the original).

The power of 'finance capital', i.e. 'capital controlled by the banks and employed by the industrialists' (p42) is so great 'in all economic and international relations that it is capable of subordinating to itself, and actually does subordinate to itself, even states enjoying complete political independence' (p74).

These are large statements and quite a lot of time could be spent on examining whether they were entirely justified even fifty years ago. Whatever the case, they carry little conviction today as descriptions of the central institutional relationships within capitalist society.

Far from being dependent on banks and similar financial institutions, industrial firms are net suppliers of finance to other sectors of the economy. Between 1949 and 1953 they disposed of one-twentieth of their accumulations or savings in this way.[5] Nor are banks too eager to take on industrial financing. According to the Radcliffe Committee[6] 'it is clear that attitudes are changing', and nevertheless they still hesitate to invest in industry except for very short periods of up to three months, and even then they do so to a limited extent: the eleven London Clearing Banks, the giants of the trade, held less than one-third of their assets in bills and advances to the private sector at the end of 1958[7] and certainly not all of this was in favour of big industrial and commercial firms. Even life assurance and pension funds, although more involved in industrial financing, are hardly in it up to their necks as yet. Their industrial investments, broadly conceived, accounted for under 40 per cent of the total in 1957 and less than half of this was in ordinary stocks and shares – the true indicator of investment.[8]

Part of the difference between Lenin's picture and the one given here stems from simple error on his part. Lenin was too impressed by conditions peculiar to Germany as documented at the time in Hilferding's *Das Finanzkapital*, and overhasty in generalizing from German evidence. It was true – it still is true to some extent – that German banks were heavily involved in industrial financing and that they wielded immense power over their clients. But German capitalism was a late developer. It found – as every backward country is finding today – that to break into the modern (in its case, British-controlled) market with backward (German) means it had to conserve every drop of saving and skill, even the very smallest, bring them together and invest them in plant bigger and better than that of their entrenched rivals. It had to make 'combined development', in Trotsky's phrase, work in its favour. Since the banks were structured around this task and since the future of German capitalism hinged on its effective performance, it is not surprising that they became the key, controlling institutions within it.

British development was different as was, to a less extent, that of American or French capitalism. Here, the scale of investment was more or less geared to the scale of accumulation. Being in the vanguard of development, rich, powerful and with no felt need to make anachronistic means perform modern tasks, British capitalism left its banks to perform their original function of lubricating industry and trade, augmenting, marginally, resources raised elsewhere (through stock markets, internal accumulations and so on) and financing international commerce. Only in their international operations did British banks come anywhere near resembling their German counterparts – but of this later.

But error accounts for only a small part of the difference between Lenin's picture and ours. Most of it is a true reflection of the changes that have occurred within capitalism itself.

Even in Britain, the banks were pretty powerful institutions at the beginning of the century, as anyone who dips into Feis's classic can learn.[9] The power was firmly based. Empire provided the British middle class with a relatively high income (see below) at the same time as it retarded the growth of British industry by providing it with a captive market.[10] Instead of being attracted towards industrial investment, middle class funds gravitated naturally towards the financial institutions (exchange banks, merchant banks, and so on) that straddled the capital-hungry backward countries and were – in the seven years preceding World War I – shunting well over half Britain's annual accumulations abroad.[11] Since the existence of a captive colonial market also retarded the concentration of British industry and its organization into gigantic units on the lines of the ones that were forming abroad, the city and its financial institutions stood out as the largest and, by reason of the international – therefore semi-political – nature of so much of its operations, the most self-conscious of capitalist institutions in the country.

But this was fifty years ago. Since then a number of things have occurred to reduce their relative stature. One is the very rapid growth that has occurred in industrial activity and in the largest industrial groups. Another is the emergence of the state as a decisive agent in the economy. Both have been touched on in a previous issue of this journal and need no repetition here.[12] Together they have shifted the locus of saving, the place where the decision to accumulate is taken – and the power to invest – to the industrial corporation and away from the financial institution.

This needs some explanation. So long as industry is expanding as it was bound to under the stimulus of two wars, and is continuing to do under that of the permanent arms economy, company directors do their best to offset increasing taxation – itself a product of wars and the arms economy – by reducing payments to shareholders. As taxation rose from 14 to 39 per cent of net company income between 1938 and 1956, dividend and interest payments fell from 68 to 35 per cent.[13] Dividends as a percentage of profits have fallen drastically this century – from 67 per cent in 1912[14] to an average no larger than 23 per cent in 1949–56.[15] They have even fallen absolutely in value – from £885 million in 1938 to £690 million in 1956 in pounds of constant purchasing power.[16] Middle class rentier incomes, i.e. incomes from property ownership, have thus fallen. At the same time, the incidence of personal taxation has encouraged them to view this development without alarm and to look to capital gains rather than income from dividends as their main source of unearned income.

But the banks have had to adapt. The flow of middle class savings which sustained their operations has been stemmed, or at least greatly reduced at source, while their control over industry and commerce has declined *pari passu* with the trend towards self-financing or financial near-autonomy in these sectors.

External factors have also clipped 'finance capital's' wings. Since the flow of private international capital has fallen drastically (see below) and public aid largely by-passes private banking channels; since, too, political independence in most of the world has broken up large currency areas into national fragments, each controlled to some degree by a Central Bank, the financial institutions which thrived above all on *international* operations have suffered[17] and been compelled in many cases to draw back. This change is nowhere more clearly shown than in the peculiar world of the City's merchant banks, once the true buccaneers of Empire. As early as 1931 the Macmillan Committee suggested that these foreign-orientated 'financial organizations concentrated in the City of London might with advantage be more closely co-ordinated with British industry'.[18] Default abroad coupled with rosier prospects at home have since amplified the message and there has been a marked shift towards domestic industrial banking. Close links have been forged with industrial groups as between Lazards and English Electric or Schroder and Pressed Steel. More typically, although more recently, this change in orientation has taken the form of amalgamation between old-established issuing houses 'disproportionately strong in foreign business' and younger firms concentrating on the 'home industrial financing which has been the mainstay of most firms which have expanded in recent years'.[19] In effect these amalgams have become managerial consultants, investment agents and brokers for the large industrial groups with which they are now associated.

3.
Capital Exports

Imperialism's dynamic was the capital exports which 'finance capital' encouraged and serviced. There is no quarrel here with Lenin. But, in his view, these capital exports were the prime index of modern capitalism. 'Under the old type of capitalism,' he wrote, 'when free competition prevailed, the export of *goods* was the most typical feature. Under modern capitalism, when monopolies prevail, the export of *capital* has become the typical feature' (p56, emphasis in original).

It is here that we part. However true it might have been of modern capitalism as seen fifty years ago, the export of capital is no more its 'typical feature' than 'finance capital' its most developed form of organization. On the contrary, the decline in the one has automatically dragged the other from its pre-eminence. Even in Britain, despite government measures designed to sustain the flow, even at the expense of growth at home; despite an accumulation of business ties and habits of generations; and despite a rate of flow – at £300 to £400 million a year in the 1950s[20] – that has scarcely ever been equalled,[21] the significance of capital exports has declined tremendously: latterly they have run at about 2 per cent of gross national product compared with 8 per cent in the period before World War I;[22] they now absorb less than 10 per cent of savings compared with some 50 per cent before;[23] and returns on foreign investment have been running at slightly over 2 per cent of national income[24] compared with 4 per cent in the 1880s, 7 per cent in 1907 and 10 per cent in 1914.[25] Between 1895 and 1913, 61 per cent of all new capital issues were on overseas account;[26] by 1938 they were down to 30 per cent and more recently accounted for no more than 20 per cent of the total.[27]

For Lenin the importance of capital exports lay in their being able to alleviate, temporarily, some of the contradictions of mature capitalism. First, the world market could cushion 'the uneven and spasmodic character of the development of individual enterprises, of individual branches of industry and individual countries (which) is inevitable under the capitalist system' (p56). Second – and this is the fundamental argument – 'The necessity of exporting capital arises from the fact that in a few countries capitalism has become "over-ripe" and (owing to the backward state of agriculture and the impoverished state of the masses) capital cannot find "profitable" investment' (p57). This argument explains why, according to Lenin, capital should, and did, flow towards backward countries. There would have been no logic in it flowing from one 'over-ripe' economy to another. Moreover,

the backward world offered singular attractions: 'In these backward countries, profits usually are high, for capital is scarce, the
price of land is relatively low, wages are low, raw materials are
cheap' (p57).

The truth of Lenin's reasoning stands or falls by his
picture of capital flows: do they really shun developed countries
and rush to backward ones ? They do not. It is notoriously difficult
to get hold of authoritative British figures but an official estimate
puts private long-term investment (*including reinvestment*) in 'less
developed areas' in recent years at 'something of the order of
£100 million' a year or between one-quarter and one-third of total
private investment abroad.[28] A similar, if less marked, bias towards developed countries is shown by US capital exports. Excluding reinvestments and stopping short before the flood of
investments in the Common Market countries occurred (both of
which would accentuate the bias) $5,238 million of private long-
term capital or 54 per cent of the total outflow of $9,769 million
went to 'high-income countries' between 1953 and 1958 inclusive
compared with $4,531 million to 'low-income countries'.[29]

It is clear that current figures simply do not bear out
Lenin's thesis. Capital does not flow overwhelmingly from mature
to developing capitalist countries. On the contrary, foreign
investments are increasingly made as between developed countries
themselves. And this is as it should be in all logic. For if we recall
the reasons Lenin advances for the export of capital we shall find
that they barely stand up to scrutiny in today's conditions.

There is no point in debating the 'cushion' argument at
any length: however important backward countries were in
absorbing the uncontrolled and disproportionate expansion of this
or that industry or sector in the heyday of Britain's industrial
supremacy and classic *laissez faire*, they play little part in doing
so today. Of the many factors in the change, political and tariff
independence in most of the world spring to mind as the most
obvious. But the most fundamental is the relatively high degree

of planning achieved in mature capitalist countries, largely as a consequence of the permanent arms economy,[30] which more or less contains the violence of sectoral expansion. The planned reduction in cotton textiles production in this country or the care with which US agricultural surpluses are disposed of in ways 'not disruptive of normal trade channels' serve to illustrate the point.

Lenin's second argument for the inevitability of capital exports – stagnation in mature capitalism – is equally difficult to sustain in the post-war period. Naturally Lenin could not have envisaged – no one in his day could conceivably have done so – the role of the permanent arms economy in stabilising mature capitalism, fixing it on a course of almost automatic growth and in transposing the locus of stagnation from mature capitalist countries to backward ones. But there it is, for one thing the major developed capitalist countries are growing at a faster rate than the major backward ones: between 1950 and 1959 percentage annual growth in the important developed countries was Japan 9·1, Germany 7·5, Italy 5·7, France 4·0, US 3·3 and Britain 2·5; for most important undeveloped ones it was Brazil 6, Congo 5, Indonesia 4, Egypt 3, India 3, Argentina 2.[31] Then again to assume (as Lenin did on the basis of a superficial measurement of railway mileage in a few colonial countries) that 'the elementary conditions for industrial development have been created' is to assume away the 'problems (crisis, agony, etc.) of the undeveloped world' we hear so much about nowadays and to believe that the $4,000 million or so of aid and long-term loans pumped into them every year from all sources arise out of a spirit of philanthropy rather than from the (probably false) belief that political stability can be achieved if only the problem of industrialization can be solved.

Lenin's third reason for capital exports – the greater profits to be had in backward countries – can also be disputed. Since foreign investments are, as will be shown below, increasingly investments in manufacturing, and manufacturing techniques are increasingly standardized the world over, with a high and fairly fixed ratio of machines to workers, the difference in profit rates that derived from the different levels in wages in developed and backward countries has tended to narrow. There are many exceptions, some of them very significant, but this is no place for detail. Suffice it that while 'current earnings on capital invested in United States manufacturing industry averaged between 15 and 20 per cent'[32] – 'the income from the United States direct investments abroad, after taxes payable to foreign governments, has in the past few years been . . . about 15 per cent.'[33] The return on US investments in countries other than Canada and Western Europe is put slightly higher – 17 per cent.[34]

4.
Colonialism

The same unreality attaches – today – to Lenin's coupling of capital exports with colonialism. Perhaps more stress ought to be laid on the interpolation 'today': physical seizure of backward areas by mature capitalist powers was so much the scheme of things at the turn of the century that there did not appear much reason to argue their connection with capital exports. Nevertheless, he did advance – rather perfunctorily – two reasons for the connexion.

One was that colonial possessions were invaluable as a haven for capital exports: 'The necessity of exporting capital also serves to stimulate the quest for colonies, for it is easier in the colonial market (and sometimes it is the only possible way), by monopolist methods to eliminate competition, to make sure of orders, to strengthen the necessary "connections," etc.' (p77). The second and by far the more important in Lenin's eyes was that colonial possessions vested control of essential raw materials in the possessor: 'The more capitalism develops, the more the need for raw materials arises, the more bitter competition becomes, and the more feverishly the hunt for raw materials proceeds all over the world, the more desperate becomes the struggle for the acquisition of colonies' (p75).

Lenin's first argument is easily refuted. His own figures for French and German foreign investments so contradicted the thesis – more than two-thirds of the French total was invested *in Europe* (p58) – that he coined a special phrase 'usury imperialism' for the one and said of the others 'in regard to Germany we have a third type' (p58). Even with regard to British 'colonial imperialism' to use Lenin's phrase, the facts do not fall into place: of the total long-term capital invested abroad, more than half (£1,983 million out of £3,763 million) was held *outside* the Empire.[35]

It would be as easy to refute the second argument by simply referring to Britain's growing import bill and shrinking colonial possessions, or to the fact that empire-shorn Germany, more than three fifths as dependent as Britain on imported industrial materials[36] has nothing like three-fifths of Britain's truncated empire to find them in. But there is more to it than refuting the equation, 'feverish-hunt-for-raw-materials' equals 'acquisition-of-colonies', Lenin's basic equation – 'the-more-capitalism-develops' equals 'the-more-the-need-for-raw-materials-arises' – is just as wrong today. Three major – and unforeseen – developments have occurred since his day. All three are inherent in the system, but their rapid maturation this generation is a product of the war-slump-war drive to autarky. One is the growing efficiency with which raw materials are used and the consequent release from the need to devote a fixed proportion of total resources to their production. It has been estimated officially for the United States that this factor alone was responsible for doubling the value of gross national product from four to eight times that of the input of raw materials consumed in the process in the first half of this century.[37] A second is the spread of industrial techniques to the production of industrial raw materials and the increasing use of 'natural' raw materials that lend themselves to industrial exploitation, like oil. Even excluding oil, any random selection will show consumption of raw materials in industrial countries increasing in the same direction as their manufactured content. While the use of crude materials in these countries increased slowly between 1950–52 and 1955–57 as follows: cotton 7 per cent, wool 12 per cent, rubber 15 per cent, jute 17 per cent and copper 20 per cent, consumption of similar processed materials, largely synthetics, rose appreciably faster: steel 31 per cent, woodpulp 33 per cent, synthetic rubber 44 per cent, aluminium 61 per cent, plastic materials 96 per cent and synthetic fibres 211 per cent.[38]

The third change in raw materials supply that has occurred since Lenin's day, one closely related to the foregoing, and one Lenin explicitly pronounced to be impossible under capitalism,[39] has been the tremendous development of agricultural production in developed countries in the West. Despite official discouragement, the average rate of growth in US agricultural production was 2·3 times as fast as the average for all other branches of activity in the 1948–58 decade;[40] in France, agricultural production rose 14 per cent annually compared with 11 per cent for industrial output between 1953 and 1958;[41] and in Western Europe generally, the current struggles on agricultural problems within and around the Common Market are a direct outcome of this industrial revolution in agriculture.

One important consequence of these developments is that capital flows that are still continuing are changing their character; from flowing into extractive industries they are being channelled increasingly towards manufacturing industries undertaken directly by the large industrial complexes that have emerged, as has been shown, at the apex of financial power in mature capitalist countries. Take India as an example: while total foreign business investments rose from Rs2,558 million in mid-1948 to Rs6,107 million at the end of 1959, or 2·4 times, investment in petroleum refining (and trading) rose from Rs223 million to

Rs1,207 million or 5·4 times, and investment in manufacturing from Rs709 million to Rs2,507 or 3·5 times. Contrast this with the record of plantation investments – an increase from Rs525 million to Rs951 million or 1·8 times – or of mining – a bare increase from Rs115 million to Rs130 million or 1·1 times.[42]

Surprisingly, Lenin did not use the strongest evidence of the link between finance capital, capital exports and colonialism available to him, viz. the importance of state and municipal bonds in total foreign investments. Those formed 30 per cent of British foreign investments in 1913 and, if certain other government-guaranteed securites were to be included, nearly one-half.[43] Arranged as they were through 'finance capital' institutions these colonial stocks constituted the most direct possible investment in empire. They too have all but disappeared. Of the £446 million of government and municipal loans outstanding to British investors in India and Ceylon in 1938, under £6 million remained by 1951,[44] the rest having been liquidated even before the 'liquidation of Empire'.

5.
End of Empire

Taking Lenin's 'last stage' literally, colonial indepen-
dence and the continuation of capitalism are incompatible. And yet we have both – in increasing quantities. Moreover, opposition to colonial independence, although evident enough in the metro-politan countries and brutal enough overseas, has had in most cases little of the spirit of the 'last ditch stand' one would expect from a society fighting for its existence. In the event it has been a relatively feeble opposition, willing to seek and abide by com-promise with national movements. There can be little doubt that changes within mature capitalism have had a lot to do with this feebleness. The decline in foreign investment and its change

from labour-using extractive industries to more capital-using manufacturing industries reduced the intake of colonial labour precisely when the impact of modern techniques was resulting in explosive increases in the colonial populations and labour forces. The old imperialist investments had probably reached their zenith by World War I and have since contributed little, if anything, to solving the colonies' mounting unemployment problems. In the meantime their stagnation and decline focussed the colonial labour movements' attacks on foreign rule, and, by negative example, sharpened their demand for an expanding economy and for the political status that might engender it. They found a potent ally in some places, like India, in the local bourgeoisie which hastened to fill the vacuum created and which found its further development hampered by foreign rule.

In its turn, colonial capital drew strength from the new forms of foreign investment. These were geared to the domestic market, interested in its expansion, in finding workers with modern skills and linking up with partners versed in local conditions – interested in fact in economic growth and the politics of growth. Even the falling off of recruitment to expatriate careers as a result of full employment at home was a factor in hastening the transfer of power: it left gaps in the administration and repressive organs of most colonial countries and led to the appointment of colonials to at least some sensitive positions.

Again, the diffusion of industrial capitalism, the decline of the imperialist powers as exporters of cheap consumer staples, together with their restrictive control of the colonies' foreign trade and economic relations, subjected them to mounting international pressure to relinquish the advantages they held in the colonies. The record is long. On the Allied side alone, it culminated during World War II, in the promise to abandon Imperial Preference as a condition of American Lend-Lease, in recurrent American demands for colonial independence as part of the post-war settlement, in a tacit Russo-American alliance to divest the older Allies of their territorial possessions and so on.

Finally, the onset of the cold war has made of independence and economic development two giant counters in a global confrontation which deals in social stability as earnestly as in missiles.

These are some of the factors in colonial independence – certainly not all. That they derived to some extent from the change in the locus and forms of accumulation, from the growing importance and changing structure of industry in mature capitalist countries and, ultimately, from the permanent arms economy is clear. It is also clear that they were not forseen, nor could have been, by Lenin and his generation.

6.
Promise and Postscript

Some of the conclusions entailed in this analysis will be taken up in later issues of *International Socialism*. There is one general statement that seems in order here, however: if good theory is operational – and this is how it should be – Lenin's *Imperialism* was supremely good theory in its day. It picked out the enemy, determined the crucial alliance, and explained what the battle was about. But the lines of battle have been redrawn and Lenin, however superb an example of the right approach to theory is no more the complete manual.

1. Page 7 of the Lawrence and Wishart edition, *Selected Works* Vol. V, to which all page references in this article relate. Emphasis has been added to the last seven words of the quotation.
2. Board of Trade, *Economic Trends*, cited in *The Times*, 2 May 1962.
3. Writing in mid-1961, U.V.Kitzinger stated: 'The last three years have also seen a vast crystallization of Franco-German

industrial agreements and measures of business integration directly provoked by the Common Market. Peugeot and Mercedes-Benz, As de Trefle and Agfa Leverkusen, Fouga and Messerschmidt, Desmarais and BV-Aral, Rhone-Poulenc and Bayer Leverkusen, Centrale de Dynamite and Hoechst, Breguet and Dornier, Lip and Holzer, Lavallette and Bosch, Manurhin and Auto-Union, Nord-Aviation and Focke-Wulf, to mention only some of the more famous names in the aeroplane and motor, chemical and mechanical industries of the two countries, have all concluded various kinds of agreement: for the exchange of patents, for manufacture under licence, for marketing of each other's products, for the joint manufacture of new products. Much the same kind of activity is going on between French firms and Belgian, Dutch and Italian firms, and almost all the combinations possible between six partners.' (*The Challenge of the Common Market*, Oxford: Basil Blackwell, 1961, pp96–7).

4. About 470 out of about 2 million private concerns in Britain (some 0·0002 per cent) accounted for 48 per cent of all paid-up capital in 1951–52 (From P.Sargant Florence, *Ownership, Control and Success of Large Companies*, London: Sweet & Maxwell 1961, Table ID p9); more than one-third of the labour force in all industrial activities work in the three largest business units – 87 per cent in cement, 84 per cent in petroleum, 93 per cent in explosives and so on (*ibid.*, Table IF, p16).

5. Brian Tew, 'Self Financing', in Tew and Henderson, *Studies in Company Finance*, London: Cambridge University Press 1959, Table 3.1, p44.

6. Committee on the Working of the Monetary System, *Report*, para. 136, p46.

7. *ibid.*, Table 8, p45.

8. *ibid.*, Tables 15, 16, pp84, 89, and p86.

9. Herbert Feis, *Europe the World's Banker 1870–1914*, Yale 1931.

10. Gross domestic capital formation fell by a quarter between 1900 and 1913 (although 1913 was the best year since 1907) while net payments abroad rose nearly seven-fold in the same period (James B. Jeffereys and Dorothy Walters, 'National Income and Expenditure of the United Kingdom, 1870–1952' in Simon Kuznets (ed), *Income and Wealth*, Series V, London: Bowes & Bowes 1955, Table XV, pp36–7).

11. *ibid.*

12. See Reform and Revolution', *International Socialism* 7 (Winter 1961–62).

13. From S.J.Prais, 'Dividend Policy and Income Appropriation', in Tew & Henderson, *op. cit.*, Table 2.1, p27.

14. J. Enoch Powell, *Saving in a Free Society*, London: Hutchinson for The Institute of Economic Affairs 1960, Table II, p29.

15. From the Treasury's *Bulletin for Industry*, no.119, April 1959.

16. S.J.Prais, *loc. cit.*, p26.

17. Notice the relief with which the Chairman of the Chartered Bank, one of the largest of those operating 'out East', greeted the decision to retain a common currency in the area beginning to be known as Malaysia: 'It must, therefore, be a matter of satisfaction that the continuance on the same parity basis, of the existing currency arrangements, to put it at the very least, postpones the fragmentation of the unified currency area comprising the Federation, Singapore and the British territories in Borneo, in which first the Straits dollar and subsequently the Malayan dollar have provided a stable and effective medium of exchange' (Statement at the Annual General Meeting, 1 April 1959).

18. Quoted in *The Economist*, 28 May 1960.

19. *The Times*, 10 February 1960.

20. The lower figure is an official estimate for 1953–59 (*Assistance from the United Kingdom for Overseas Development*, Cmnd 974, March 1960, p6), the higher is a private estimate for 1956–57 (A.R.Conan, *Capital Imports into Sterling Countries*, London: Macmillan 1960, p84).

21. Between 1885 and 1895, capital exports from Britain average some £30 million, and during the following decade – some £40 million (*Problems of International Investment*, London: RIIA 1938, p115) or in terms of today's prices, about £100 million annually over the whole period. Only between 1905 and 1913 did they become heavy – some £200 million a year – but even then they did not reach the £150 million mark – roughly the current rate in real terms – until 1910 (C.K.Hobson cited in Conan, *op. cit.*, p82). Feis (*op. cit.*, pp14–15) gives lower figures however: £185 million annual average for 1910–13.

22. Using Feis's conservative estimate for capital exports (see previous note).

23. Feis, *op. cit.*, pp5, 14–15.

24. Annual average of 'net income from abroad' for 1953–56 as given in the Blue Books of *National Income and Expenditure* plus an estimated £200 million as given in *The Times*, 24 April 1958.

25. Feis, *op. cit.*, p16; Jenks (*The Migration of British Capital to 1875*, London: Jonathan Cape 1938, pp5–6) gives a figure of 20 per cent for 1914.

26. From A.R.Hall, 'A Note on the English Capital Market . . .', *Economica*, February 1957, p62.

27. UN, *The International Flow of Private Capital, 1956–1958*, New York, 1959, p51.

28. *Assistance . . . op. cit.*, p6.

29. United Nations, *op. cit.*, Table 3, p20.

30. See 'Reform and Revolution', *loc. cit.*

31. United Nations, *World Economic Survey 1960*, New York 1961, Tables 1-1, 2-1, pp16, 58.

32. United Nations, *Measures for the Economic Development of Under-Developed Countries*, New York 1951, p19.

33. United Nations, *The International Flow of Private Capital 1946–1952*, New York 1954, p16.

34. *ibid.*, footnote.

35. From Feis, *op. cit.*, Table on p23.

36. H.H.Liesner, *The Import Dependence of Britain and Western Germany*, Princeton Studies in International Finance, no.7, Princeton 1957, Table 25, p37.

37. US Department of Commerce, Bureau of the Census, *Raw Materials in the United States Economy*, Working Paper no.1, Washington DC, 1954.

38. NIESR cited in *Barclays Bank Review*, February 1961.

39. He wrote: 'It goes without saying that *if capitalism could develop agriculture*, which today lags far behind industry everywhere, if it could raise the standard of living of the masses . . . there could be no talk of a superfluity of capital. . . . *But if capitalism did these things it would not be capitalism . . .*' (pp56–7 emphasis added).

40. Andrew Shonfield, *The Attack on World Poverty*, London: Chatto & Windus 1960, p176.

41. K.S.Karol, 'A View of De Gaulle's France', *New Statesman*, 17 February 1961.

42. 'Foreign Investments in India', Reserve Bank of India *Bulletin*, April 1960, Statement IV; and an article of the same name in the RBI *Bulletin*, May 1961, Statement II.

More than half the increase in plantation investments was accounted for by paper revaluations of assets in the mid-1950s.

43. From Feis, *op. cit.*, Table, p27.

44. Phillip W. Bell, *The Sterling Area in the Postwar World*, Oxford 1956, Table LX, pp370–2.

7. International Capitalism

The rash of political independence in the colonial world since World War II has more than once strained the concepts used by socialists and even, sometimes, their credulity. Does it mean the end of imperialism? If it does, how are we to explain the great power coercion that is so central a feature of our time? If it does not, what is the hidden common feature between imperialism today and that of a generation ago?

This article is an attempt to answer these and some related questions. It skirts around many problems: cold war is not mentioned; nor is the structure of international coercion – western and eastern – built around it. The immediate future of economic, social and political developments in ex-colonial countries is hardly touched upon; and so with the role of proletariat and peasantry. The view given is a drastically foreshortened one of broad trends that have affected European imperialism over the past half-century.

1.

Classic Imperialism

It is as well to recall the main features of pre-1914 imperialism. At the same time, in order to keep the discussion free of some of the more draughty generalizations, it is equally as well to confine it to one country, such as India, jewel of the British Imperial Crown, concentrating on those aspects of her relations with Britain which were typical of the system as a whole.

By the beginning of this century, 'India had come to be regarded as a plantation of England, growing raw products to be shipped by British agents in British ships, to be worked into fabrics by British skill and capital and to be re-exported to India by British merchants in India through their British agents.'[1] That India had come to be so regarded was no accident. A lot of British effort had gone into wrenching the colonial economy into rough complementarity with that of the imperialist; and a lot of British capital had come to ensure that it remained that way. How much is difficult to say. Estimates of investments prior to World War I are so unreliable as not to be worth giving,[2] but whatever the precise figure there is no doubt that British capital concentrated almost exclusively on supplying British industry's demand for raw materials, either by producing or transporting them. An *Economist* report in 1911 covering India and Ceylon attributed 60 per cent of investments to tea and rubber plantations, 12·3 per cent to tramways, electricity and other utilities, 8·9 per cent to vegetable oils, 5·7 per cent to finance, 2·7 per cent to shipping and 3·7 per cent to commercial and industrial undertakings.[3] In other words slightly more than three-quarters were in the extractive industries that dominated India's exports at the time and most of the rest in the means of transporting them to their foreign markets.

Characteristic of this type of investment was its use of large quantities of unskilled labour with a minute lacing of fixed capital and technically qualified management. Equally characteristic was its utter dependence on efficient contact with markets abroad: swift and reliable transportation from the point of production via the ports to London and a flexible banking system to transmit the proceeds of sales, provide seasonal loans to cover shipment, and so on. In effect this meant that it could not have taken place without the prior intervention of the colonial state; nor could it have sustained itself without that state's unremitting efforts at keeping the conditions of colonial exploitation unchanged. It was the £20,000 a year special subsidy from the East India Company which enabled the P & O line to inaugurate and maintain a regular shipping service between India and Europe from 1841; it was the officially guaranteed-interest railway contracts signed initially at the close of that decade that ended in linking India's hinterland with her ports and so, ultimately, with Britain. Although 'the solid core of pressure both for steam navigation and for railways came from the great mercantile houses of London and the other leading British ports trading to India and China',[4] their existence was organized and underwritten by the state or its equivalent of the day. So it was with the supply of labour to the uphill plantations, with the fixing of the rupee exchange rate to facilitate the free flow of funds between Calcutta and London, and much besides.

So necessary was economic activity by the state in perpetuating the system that it became a major sphere of investment in its own right: well over half the foreign capital in India in 1926–27 was held in government stock,[5] and the proportion hardly changed until World War II when the official debt abroad was refunded.

That the state subserves business goes without further comment to readers of this journal. But there were two things that distinguished the type of service rendered by the colonial state: first, as suggested by the examples given, was its commitment to keeping the country open to foreign trade and foreign investment. Nothing was allowed to impair the forced complementarity between the home and host economies. Protection for nascent industry was unthinkable; an independent currency or any form of exchange control to stop the drain of profits abroad inconceivable. *Laissez faire* in a colony's external relations became a moral imperative for the imperial ruling class, as rapacious as any.[6] Not so with regard to economic activity *within* a colony. There the second special service was, paradoxically, to preserve private foreign capital's monopoly. The export industries it favoured normally made few demands on skill or fixed investment. They could be, and have been, readily assimilated by the local population, as in the case of rubber production in Indonesia, tea growing in parts of India, and so on. Were it not for the rigging of railway rates to encourage traffic to and from the ports at the expense of internal traffic, the denial of even the most elementary technical education to the subject people and a host of similar discriminatory acts and non-acts, foreign private capital's preponderance would have been shortlived. As it was, its special relation with the colonial state plus its even more closely guarded monopoly of the service of British banks, issuing houses and other paraphernalia of private capitalism were sufficient to ensure that the commanding heights of the capitalist sector remained in its hands: as late as the 1940s, well beyond the period of classic imperialism, about 85 per cent of the total area planted to tea – a major export – was British-controlled, as were 85 per cent of the jute industry, 70 per cent of coal mining,[7] 80 per cent of foreign trade,[8] etc., etc.

A natural corollary was for the state machine to be kept free of local infiltration. It was not until 1919, after the shock of war and the first thrusts of the nationalist movement that a minority of posts in the Indian Civil Service were opened to Indians and examinations held in the country; as late as 1923 the Lee Commission recommended Indianization in the Service at a rate that would ensure only 50 per cent Indian membership by 1939.

What happened outside the modern sector was of little direct concern to the foreign power. If the maintenance of Pax Britannica could be eased by recourse to local, landowning or feudal authority, as happened in India once the 1857 Mutiny had demonstrated how astronomic was to be the cost of bedding foreign rule in every pore of the country, well and good. 'Progressive' capitalism was never loth to cut costs by combining with the most benighted and reactionary elements anywhere. Indeed, where colonial countries were concerned, the stronger the feudal landowners and the more influence they wielded over the nascent bourgeoisie, turning it into the cowardly, uninspired class bereft of initiative which it so commonly is in such countries, the better for foreign capital. Were it left entirely to its foreign counterpart and local feudalism, local capital might expect to become, at best, a broker between foreign capital and domestic society, a 'compradore' bourgeoisie without productive resources of its own.

These bones of description do not pretend to embody the complex system that contained the pre-1914 world. They might, however, be enough to support a crude description of the class conflicts and the class alliances typical of it.

At least until the inter-war years in India, it was exceptional for the few industrial workers to be employed by native-born bosses. It was natural for them to associate the brutalities of capitalist exploitation, in both private and public sectors, with foreign rule. The peasant too was constantly being hurled against the twin pillars of foreign power. The state exacted taxes; ruined his handicrafts by opening the country to Lancashire cottons; did nothing to stop the drain of peasant wealth as the terms of trade index for primary commodities dropped from 163 in the late 1870s to 137 in 1913,[9] refused to encourage the industries that might have solved the growing problem of rural unemployment. Private foreign capital actually brought them the cottons, bought their produce and sometimes held them virtual prisoners on its plantations under the most appalling conditions. Finally, the nascent bourgeoisie pressed vainly towards the industries which it was technically qualified to undertake. Starved of state support, driven from the sources of loan capital, largely excluded from European trade associations, discriminated against by officials and business, denied access to government and administration, its potential growth became a political matter, hingeing on freedom from British rule.

This is not to deny that many indigenous capitalists – notably some Parsi houses in India – flourished under British rule; or that the three classes singled out here were not the entirety of Indian society; or that they found themselves in deepest conflict *inter se* on more than one occasion. The picture is infinitely more complex than appears here. Nevertheless, one thing seems incontrovertible and is borne out by the experience of the time: imperialist rule so stunted the growth of modern productive forces, so pinioned economic development, that these three crucial classes were forced willy nilly into a loose nationalist coalition with the overriding aim of ridding the country of foreign rule.

For long – so long as classic imperialism was an expanding system – this nationalist coalition made heavy weather. Its major frontal assault on imperialism in India – the Swadeshi movement of 1905–8 – petered out as the dependence of India's modern sector on Britain was brought home in practice to the boycotters. But slowly the conditions of struggle changed. Imperceptible at first, something was happening to the system which robbed it of its dynamic and made it increasingly vulnerable to nationalist attack.

2.
The Arms Economy

It is time to turn back to the imperialist countries whose dynamics and organization formed the guts of revolutionary socialist analysis before and during World War I. Since Lenin's *Imperialism* is the most well-known it can best serve as a framework of reference in what follows.

Lenin's definition of imperialism embraced 'the following five essential features:

'1 – The concentration of production and capital developed to such a stage that it creates monopolies which play a decisive role in economic life.

'2 – The merging of bank capital with industrial capital and the creation, on the basis of "finance capital", of a financial oligarchy.

'3 – The export of capital, which has become extremely important, as distinguished from the export of commodities.

'4 – The formation of international capitalist monopolies which share the world among themselves.

'5 – The territorial division of the whole world among the greatest capitalist powers is completed.'[10]

There is no doubt of the primacy of Lenin's first 'feature', both in reality and in his exposition. Were it not for the concentration and accumulation of capital in ever larger (and fewer) units, a process inherent in capitalism from its inception, none of the other features of this 'highest stage' could have emerged. It would be an academic exercise to spend time on substantiating this; few would deny that monopolization and its attendant – the internationalization of monopolies (Lenin's fourth 'feature') – are still with us, and more pronounced than ever.

It is only when we come to the others that we begin to question the validity of Lenin's thesis today. 'Finance capital'? Its export? Territorial division? . . . Are these still operative? Or at least do they still have anything like the significance attributed to them at the beginning of the century?

Some idea of the close association of the colonial state with colonial business has been given. It does not take much to realize that it had its counterpart in the imperialist countries themselves. Would-be imperialisms like German or Japanese capital, faced with the final territorial division of the world, could hope to prosper only by conquest, through the agency of their state. Existing imperialisms could continue to do so only by organizing their defence – again through the state. The strengthening of the state, its closer functional integration with big business, the growing militarization of the economy have demonstrably become the normal condition of capitalist existence. To say this, or that the violence of world war and its political and economic organization are characteristic of our generation, is to draw attention to the experience of our generation. It needs no proof. All that will be attempted here is a sketch of some of the changes that have accompanied and resulted from the emergence of the permanent arms economy.

In the first place demands were made of manufacturing output which were new in scale. Manufacturing as such has become more important: in Britain, it accounted for 42 per cent of gross fixed investment in 1960 compared with 32 per cent in 1938.[11] Within industry it is heavy manufacturing and particularly the giant metal-using and chemical combines that have grown fastest: between 1949 and 1955 the hundred largest industrial companies in Britain increased their share of all industrial profits from 25·2 to 31·5 per cent;[12] they were growing at a rate of 12·1 per cent compound per year compared with 6·8 per cent for all industrial companies.[13]

Second, wartime disruption of international trade, the need for every ounce of production to satisfy the gaping scarcities opened up by the slaughter and the real concessions that nationalist movements could exact in the circumstances, led to a rash of industrialization in hitherto virgin areas. In India, cotton and jute production expanded rapidly during World War I, steel production rose from 91,000 tons in 1913 to 124,000 in 1918,[14] glass manufacturing took root.[15] The paid-up capital of all joint-stock companies rose 3·3 times between 1913 and 1921–22; average dividends in some industrial firms rose as high as 200 per cent.[16] Not all the gains were lost during the interwar depression and Indian industry managed to hang on until World War II brought relief in the form of the greatest boom in its history: between 1937 and 1945 production went up 20 per cent in cotton textiles, 43 per cent in steel, 34 per cent in chemicals, 97 per cent in cement and in paper. The general index rose not less than 20 per cent.[17] The subsequent progress of industry under the Plans – coincidental with world rearmament – is too well known to need repeating.

Unlimited markets at home coupled with growing competition abroad encouraged the expanding industrial sector in mature capitalist economies to finance more and more of its own expansion: in 1912, 67 per cent of company profits were distributed to shareholders, in 1922, 53 per cent, in 1957–8, 27 per cent.[18] The 1949–56 annual average was as low as 23 per cent.[19] Here again, war and the spread of industry abroad were instrumental not only in forcing the process whereby the industrial giants became the leading *potential* accumulators of society's surplus, but in acting *directly* on their dividend policy and so making them in practice the prime centres of accumulation. It demanded mighty increases in taxation, which bore most heavily on personal incomes as opposed to profits; its totality and the consequent need for 'national unity' softened ruling class resistance to social reform which again needed to be underpinned by a significant rise in 'welfare' expenditure (financed from more taxation) and by an ostensible egalitarianism in official policy which, in its turn, meant dividend restraint amongst other things under the Labour government and an increasingly severe tax on distributed profits ever since. These combined with other factors – growth of professional management, conditioned behaviour derived from one-and-a-half decades of capital issues control, and many others – to reduce the outflow of dividends absolutely since pre-war, from £885 million in 1938 to £690 million in 1956 in pounds of constant purchasing power.[20]

The surge of the industrial corporation and relative eclipse of individual middle-class capital accumulations and, notably, its typical 'finance capital' institutions such as commercial and merchant banks are obvious. The 'institutionalization' of such accumulations and their growing concentration in life assurance and pension funds (which account for the major part of new personal savings);[21] the growing involvement of such funds in industrial financing to the extent that, despite some legal inhibitions which have recently been cleared away,[22] they took up more securities in industrial companies in 1957 than the combined capital issues of those companies;[23] the spate of mergers between ancient internationally- and commercially-orientated merchant banks and the brash new domestic finance houses engaged in industrial investment . . . all these merely serve to underline one fact. Stated again, it is that the large concentrations of capital are no longer in the hands of banks and the other finance capital institutions as they were in the days of classic imperialism, when analysed by Luxemburg, Lenin or Hilferding, but in those of the large industrial corporations in which technical, productive and financial power are fused.

3.
Changes in World Markets

The implications reach too far into the nature of contemporary capitalism to be more than partially and superficially mentioned. Perhaps most important internationally is that the war-engendered drive to self-sufficiency in food and raw materials has boosted the spontaneous thrust of these manufacturing giants towards exploiting their industrial techniques in these fields, and towards the increasing use of materials which lend themselves to such exploitation. The use of oil at the expense of coal is merely a better-known result of this displacement of 'natural', unprocessed raw materials by 'manufactured' ones. There are many other examples: the consumption of new, largely synthetic materials in Britain between 1950–52 and 1955–57 increased by 31 per cent for steel, 33 per cent for woodpulp, 44 per cent for synthetic rubber, 46 per cent for petroleum, 61 per cent for aluminium, 96 per cent for plastic materials and 211 per cent for synthetic fibres, as compared with increases in the use of comparable old materials of 7 per cent for cotton, 12 per cent for wool, 15 per cent for natural rubber, 17 per cent for jute and 20 per cent for copper.[24] As far as food production is concerned, the recent breakthrough on the farm of industrial techniques in western capitalist countries is well illustrated by the fact that the growth of productivity in US agriculture in the 1948–58 decade was, despite official dampers, 2·3 times as rapid as the average for all other branches of activity;[25] or that in the 1953–58 period in France, the annual increase in agricultural output averaged 14 per cent compared with a figure for industrial production of 11 per cent.[26]

Add to these trends the general saving in raw materials affected by both greater engineering efficiency and the shift to more capital intensive and technologically intensive products which, in the US, has meant that the value of gross output in 1950 was 8 times that of the raw materials used compared with 4 times in 1900,[27] and the relative decline in international trade in crude raw materials becomes apparent. As apparent should be the decline in the importance of the colonial primary products' producers for developed capitalism, the loss in complementarity between backward and mature countries and the loss in importance of those institutions – private or state – which perpetuated that complementarity in practice.

Before continuing this line of thought, two international implications of the shift in the internal power structure of capital should be made explicit. First, the nature of the capitalist market and the importance of the military budget in it, together with the relative growth of accumulations in the keeping of giant industrial corporations, have reduced the volume of investment undertaken abroad – capital exports – to a shadow of its former self. As has already been shown in this magazine,[28] they have been estimated

at an average of £300–400 million a year from Britain in the
1950s,[29] which, although larger than they have ever been over a
comparable period,[30] is certainly of trifling significance compared
with the pre-World War I situation: then they constituted 8 per
cent of gross national product,[31] now some 2 per cent;[32] then
they accounted for some 50 per cent of all saving,[33] now some
8–11 per cent;[34] then returns on foreign investment formed 4 per
cent of national income in the 1880s, 7 per cent in 1907 and 10
per cent in 1914,[35] now they amount to just over 2 per cent.[36]
Between 1895 and 1913, some 61 per cent of all new capital
issues for investment were on overseas account;[37] by 1938 they
accounted for 30 per cent and more recently for no more than
20 per cent of the total.[38] The figures and the proportions differ
from country to country, but the overall trend has been the same,
being steeper for capital exports to backward countries than
amongst developed ones.

Second, such capital exports as still take place are very
different from what they were. Gone are the individual portfolio
investments, handled by banks and other financial intermediaries,
which accounted for more than 90 per cent of Britain's overseas
holdings in 1914;[39] they had been reduced to some 16 per cent
of all new foreign investments between 1954 and 1957.[40] Gone
is the heavy investment in government stock – some £1,000
million in the Commonwealth alone before World War II; by
1956 these holdings had fallen to £500 million in pounds of one-
half to one-third the value.[41] Foreign investment, especially in
backward countries, is now the business of a small number of
corporations – no more than one-half of one per cent in the
United States[42] – whose size and whose 'mix' of know-how,
productive and financial resources needs no state aid to constitute
a monopoly. Such investment is typically *direct* and takes the
form of the wholly-controlled subsidiaries which accounted for
86 per cent of total British foreign investment in 1958.[43]

India gives striking confirmation of these changes. At

least half of British private investment was withdrawn between
the outbreak of World War II and the first few months of Independence;[44] since then and up to the end of 1956, while foreign
investment in manufacturing (including oil refining) rose by more
than 170 per cent, in tea plantations they rose by a little over half
(largely due to a book revaluation of existing assets), fell absolutely
in mining, trading (except in oil), and stagnated or gained very
slightly in most other traditional fields of investment.[45] The same
process is taking place *within* the big international companies:
'Ten years ago', wrote the senior research office of Unilever's giant
subsidiary, the United Africa Company,

> we were primarily concerned with produce and the
> importing of so-called "staple" commodities. Today
> these activities are of dwindling importance, and our
> capital and managerial energies are mainly directed
> towards local industry and the importing, distribu-
> tion and servicing of the more difficult and technical
> type of goods – from cold storage products to bull-
> dozers and television sets.[46]

And even such unbelievably pure examples of the old pattern as
the American United Fruit Company and its sterling subsidiary,
Fyffes, are shifting their operations: from bananas exclusively to
bananas plus bauxite and oil; and within their banana empire,
'the new policy is to hang on to the distribution of bananas, but
let the nationals of the banana republics take over growing as
soon as possible.'[47]

The contrast with classic imperialism could scarcely be
sharper: where there were once a large number of individual
investors abroad, new investments are typically made by a few
giant, mainly manufacturing, concerns; where the many small
accumulations were heavily dependent on financial intermediaries
like banks, the large concentrations of investible surpluses are
now autonomously controlled; where capital exports were essential
to complement the metropolitan productive structure, extensively
as it were, this rounding or completing of the productive structure

is now intensive, built into the economy; where such capital exports were large absolutely and larger in their relative importance to the capitalist economy, they are now small; where they took the form of technically unsophisticated and labour-intensive industries, new investments are now typically the opposite; where, therefore, foreign control of the state was essential to their proper functioning, this is no longer true. The antonyms could be multiplied. The thing to be remembered about them is that they contrast ideal types, the limits to which real examples tend but which they probably never fully resemble.

4.

Capital becomes International

The new investments are inherently monopolistic. The techniques and resources they deploy abroad make redundant institutional restrictions on potential local rivals and therewith, in backward countries, many of the central functions of the colonial state. On the contrary, their bias towards manufacturing, towards the local market, coupled with the decay in the old division of labour between the home and host economies impel them towards protection, state intervention and all the normal aids to industrialization. To put it generally, the loose integration with the host economy which was so cardinal a feature of foreign capital a generation or two ago, its enclave character, can no longer meet its requirements in backward countries today; it needs to be replaced by a much closer relationship. Then it was a matter of exporting capital; now, if it is to succeed – a big 'if' this – it has to export capitalism.

The class implications of this shift in foreign interest are enormous. Where before competition overshadowed all other elements in the relations between foreign and domestic capital, the latter chafing under a mountain of restrictions and frustrations;

now, after independence, despite many points of friction and competition that remain, the overriding element is one of mutual dependence and convenience. Local capital is inheriting the labour intensive industries vacated by its foreign counterpart; it is proving itself indispensable in mediating between the complex foreign unit and its environment: in handling labour, supplies, sales, relations with the state; it is showing subtlety in its use of that state beyond anything that could have been achieved by an alien bureaucracy. In a word, it is functioning in a way and on a level necessary for modern foreign capital, but impossible for it to emulate directly. In its turn, it is buttressed by its foreign partner in a way that would have been unthinkable fifty years ago. The vast flow of state aid that crosses into backward countries every year – some $4–5,000 million a year in economic aid alone – is part of the return; technical and financial collaboration in private and state industrial projects is another part.

In some cases – one of which is India – a local agent able and willing to enter such a partnership was easily found. In others – and here most of Africa stands witness – there was nothing for it but to create one in the form of a state bureaucracy. Whether the purposes of foreign capital are best served by one or the other; whether one or other is intrinsically more suited to achieving mature, industrial capitalism within the time permitted today; whether orthodox western capitalism *can* collaborate with a form of state capitalism in backward countries over the long term or, conversely, state capitalism *à la russe* adapt to more orthodox models abroad are strategic questions. Unfortunately they reach beyond the scope of this article. All that can be done here is draw some of the conclusions that derive for socialists from the spontaneous withdrawal of classic imperialism and from its new relationship to the indigenous ruling class in backward countries whatever the precise form of internal organization adopted by the latter.

One reservation need be made, however. It is easier to

write of spontaneous withdrawals than to see them in practice. It would be a sorry history of the transfer of power in India that did not refer to the mighty wave of strikes that swept through the country at the end of World War II or that ignored the decisive role played by the mutiny in the Royal Indian Navy. More recently the seven-year bloodbath in Algeria, Suez, Cuba and now South Vietnam look anything but a spontaneous withdrawal as does the near-apoplexy that seized large sections of the Tory party in this country whenever Central Africa was mentioned. There is a moral too in the encroaching forest in the Congo. Even though the gathering forces of nationalist revolt might succeed in precipitating 'spontaneous withdrawal', peaceful transfer to an indigenous ruling class might not be fore-ordained – it might not be ready to have such greatness thrust upon it. There is indeed an infinity of reservation and qualification with which the thesis of spontaneous withdrawal should be read, but there is equally a sense in which the thesis is valid: capitalism has undergone a transformation which enabled it to withstand, however unwillingly, the loss of its colonies, without disaster, without indeed, much dislocation or discomfort; which has enabled it, in most cases, to work, however grudgingly, for a relatively peaceful transfer of stewardship to a local ruling class. It is this broad process whose roots and some of whose implications have been detailed above. It is a long-term, historic process whose more precise implications for socialist theory and policy need now be looked at.

5.

Implications for Socialists

It hardly seems necessary to sum up one's disagreement with Lenin on imperialism, as he defined it, as the 'highest stage of capitalism'. However correct the analysis in his day, and however justified the conclusions – and these are essentially true even in retrospect – it must be rejected on at least four counts: *finance capital* is not nearly as important for and within the system as it was; the *export of capital* is no longer of great importance to the system; *political control* in the direct sense meant by Lenin is rapidly becoming dated; and finally, resulting from these, we don't have imperialism but we still have capitalism . . . If anything, it is the permanent war and arms economies that are 'the highest stage of capitalism'.

Indeed, it is difficult to see what value there is in still using the word imperialism to describe the system of big power aggression and coercion of today unless it lies in the reassurance to be derived from familiar sounds. The one feature held in common by all imperialisms to date – Roman, Tsarist or British – was their direct control of the state in subject territories. Today such control is rapidly becoming vestigial, and the distinction between empire and colony which loomed so large half a century ago increasingly irrelevant, politically and economically. Still very embryonic, the picture forming slowly, vaguely, but surely before our eyes is one of a far more homogeneous world in which many centres of capital and many more potential ones – some large and powerful, others weak and willing, yet independent – jostle and compete, forming, dissolving and reforming alliances of expediency where before division of labour and the labour of divisions imposed an immutable pattern of relationships. Again, there is reason to enter the qualifications already made: it might well require revolution to turn an ex-colony into an independent centre of capital; and again imperialism is still very real – in Southeast Asia, Central and Southern Africa, and elsewhere; armed with modern techniques it is more horrific than it ever was. All one is saying – and the recent collapse of the dinosaurs in Algeria and Cuba underlines the fact – is that it is dying as reality and therefore as a useful concept.

This is more than a matter of definition. The frustrations

of a potential local ruling class, the destruction of the peasantry and the exploitation of the new, colonial working class inherent in classic imperialism entailed, as has been shown, a loose but real national coalition. True, within the coalition the working class was assigned a role of special significance – as in Lenin's 'revolutionary-democratic dictatorship of the proletariat and peasantry' or in Trotsky's theory of permanent revolution – but it was at best a substitutive one, devolving upon it by default, because the local bourgeoisie could not develop beyond client status, could not be other than an 'inconsistent bourgeoisie' in Lenin's phrase. Trotsky too saw the roots of proletarian leadership in backward countries in negative terms: a result of the compromises with feudalism indulged in by the bourgeoisie, of the uneven development of the bourgeoisie and proletariat in such countries, a result, to take it back one further step, of uneven development on a world scale. The underlying assumption, whether for Trotsky with his uncompromising proletarianism, or for Lenin with his peasant-worker alliance (in theory at least until the revolution), or for the Mensheviks with their crude united front of all 'new' classes (the model for Stalinist tactics in backward countries ever since), or for the hosts of revolutionaries and pseudo-revolutionaries in other countries this last generation, was undoubtedly the objective unity of all major classes in the struggle against imperialism and for independence, the framework within which they could grow.

The thesis of this article is that the conditions that gave the assumption validity have changed. To repeat, the national bourgeoisie – or failing it, the national bureaucracy – has been rescued from oblivion by imperialism's withdrawal; national independence has come to it, in many cases without a struggle and therewith have come the levers of economic development and its own growth; finally it has gained greatly in strength from foreign capital's new need for willing and active partners in production and from the associated flow of cold war aid. To say, then, that the local bourgeoisie or bureaucracy has opted out of the national coalition, or is in the process of doing so, is to state the obvious. Less obvious perhaps are the conclusions to be derived.

First, and most important, where before the working class could expect to rely on allies – fitful and weak though they always were – in the struggle against foreign rule, now in the countries that have gained political independence, their struggle is more specifically a *class* struggle directed against capital as such, foreign and domestic. Where foreign capital is overwhelmingly the major component this class struggle is bound to have nationalist overtones. But here the working class is in no way a substitute leadership, its nationalism is a *class* expression, in the teeth of rather than in default of, the local bourgeoisie. In such conditions any policy based on the creation of a 'single national democratic front' as at the 1961 Communist Party of India Congress at Vijaywada must be rejected absolutely.[48] So must its obverse in the developed countries: the blanket defence and tortuous apologetics placed at the service of 'national leaders' and their regimes by the institutions of the labour movement. Nehru's arrest of 15,000 strikers in the first few hours of a national civil service strike in 1960, or Nkrumah's regimentation of the Ghanaian labour movement, or Ben Bella's and Castro's are as grim instances of class oppression as any. To keep silent is to condone them.

This is a plea to assimilate the 'new countries' into the traditional framework of class analysis. But it is more than that. It is an affirmation that national solutions to, say, cold war, are becoming increasingly unrealistic and class solutions increasingly necessary. It is a rejection of the many attempts, call them positive neutralism, some forms of Third Campism, or whatever, to find refuge from Great Power terror in alliances of 'uncommitted countries'. A country like India that demands – and obtains – one-quarter or more of its Plan outlay from both camps might seem independent of either. In reality it thrives on their competition. In reality the stability of its ruling class depends on the continuance of their ruling classes. It is inconceivable that India or any in the growing ranks of cold war brokers would endanger the stability of their regimes by opting for cold war isolationism.

Finally: when the continued functioning of capitalism rested so largely on Empire and when the form of operations abroad was such as to ultimately range almost the entire colonial population against the foreign occupation, there was good reason to believe that capitalism as a world system was most vulnerable where it was least acceptable, in the colonies; and there was a case for concentrating the revolutionary movement's energies as much as possible on the struggle for national independence. These, at least, were the underlying theoretical considerations – in addition to the ebb of revolution in Europe which was, of course, infinitely more convincing – in the Comintern's shift of attention to colonial issues at its second Congress in July 1920 and in its convening of the 'First Congress of Peoples of the East' in Baku later that year.

The thesis is untenable today. However vulnerable certain segments of the capitalist class to events abroad and however influential they be, metropolitan capital as a whole is scarcely dependent on its marginal investments in backward countries; the economic ties that remain are less ties between functionally-integrated and distinct units than they were and more ties of ownership, i.e. legalistic ones, between similar and, therefore, functionally independent productive units. Put differently, the loss of a typical imperialist investment would have upset the home economy of which it was an operative part where a similar loss today, affecting a typical modern investment (with the partial, though important, exception of oil), would have merely a quantitative effect, reducing the resources of metropolitan capitalism but not affecting its pattern of production. Developed capitalism is thus less vulnerable economically to attack in backward countries. At the same time, by reason of the new alliance formed around the new type of international investment, capitalism in backward countries is more resistant to attack from within. This is not to say it is stable or that it can continue in its present form for any length of time. It might well be that the only form in which it can triumph in large sections of the world is through state initiative – bureaucratic state capitalism – and the destruction of its bourgeois democratic cousin and rival. It might be that the capitalism we know in the 'western' and 'neutral' parts of the backward world will founder on its inability to solve the agrarian problem and the unemployment problem in that world without a degree of social regimentation and political isolation for which it is unsuited in its present form. The importance of these questions to every particular of labour movement tactics in backward countries is obvious, but whatever the reply the proposition remains unaltered, namely, that having become more firmly based on an alliance between the indigenous ruling class in politically independent countries and the metropolitan ruling class, capital is less vulnerable to working class attack in backward countries than it was. Unstable it might be: workers and peasants are working up to modern demands and forms of struggle – a kind of 'demonstration effect' is operating. But the lag between capitalist internationalism and working class internationalism acts effectively to insulate their struggles. In sum, to believe nowadays that the short route to revolution in London, New York or Paris lies through Calcutta, Havana, or Algiers, is to pass the buck to where it has no currency. To act on this belief is to rob the revolutionary socialist movement of the few dollars it still possesses.

In the most general terms – and here is where the article started – the transition from imperialism to an arms economy in the mature capitalist countries has corroded a system in which backward countries fulfilled a special function in the world capitalist economy; in which, consequently, revolutionary strategy differed significantly from place to place. It has speeded up the export of capitalism and the assimilation of its major class features in a growing proportion of the world and diminished the scope for a political programme not based four-square on class analysis and working-class interests. There are exceptions of course – white South Africa's colonialist economy has proved strong enough to absorb and assimilate the new trends, and revolutionary strategy should still orientate on some form of national coalition under working-class leadership; Portuguese power in Africa is ferociously old-model imperialist; and so on. In these the traditional analysis still holds in part and the traditional weapons retain a lot of their edge. But in the bulk of the old empires new conditions obtain. They demand a practical internationalism based on the growing uniformity in the conditions of exploitation, the growing irrelevance of national struggles as such, the growing fusion of national and class struggles and the growing similarity in the immediate aims of the working class the world over. The greatest service we can render international socialism is to help stoke up the fires at home.

1. Mover of the Swadeshi (home production) Resolution adopted at the Allahabad convention of the Indian National Congress in 1910.

2. The first estimate not patently false is Dr V.K.R.V.Rao's, relating to 1926–27. It puts total British private investment at just over £150 million.

3. *The Economist*, 21 June 1911, p1345. Government and railway securities are excluded.

4. Daniel Thorner, *Investment in Empire*, Philadelphia 1950, p23.

5. Rao, *op. cit.*, cited in *Census of India's Foreign Liabilities and Assets*, Reserve Bank of India (RBI), Bombay 1950, p153.

6. Philip Woodruff described what happened in the matter of famine relief. In 1866 the crops failed in the Indian province of Orissa. The members of the Board of Revenue who advised the Lieutenant-Governor were, he wrote in his book, *The Guardians*, ' "held by the most rigid rules of the direct political

economy". They rejected "almost with horror" the idea of importing grain. They would not even allow the authorities in Orissa to take the grain from a ship which ran ashore on their coast in March. It was bound for Calcutta and to Calcutta the grain must go. In fact, it rotted in the holds while plans were made to move it . . . By the time relief came a quarter of the population were dead.' (Quoted by John Strachey in *The End of Empire*, London 1959, pp55–56.)

7. *Notes on the Rise of the Business Communities in India*, Gokhale Institute of Politics and Economics, New York: Institute of Pacific Relations 1951 (cyclostyled), pp6, 10, 20, 45.

8. J.J.Pardiwalla, *Exchange Banks in India*, Bombay (thesis typescript), p31.

9. *Economic Development of Under-Developed Countries, Relative Prices of Primary Products and Manufactures in International Trade*, United Nations, E/2544, 1953, p22.

10. *Selected Works*, Vol. V, London 1936, p81.

11. *National Income and Expenditure 1957*, London: HMSO, Table 50, and *The Economist*, 8 April 1961, p148. For technical reasons manufacturing is aggregated with contracting and some distribution.

12. S.J.Prais, 'Size, Growth and Concentration', in *Studies in Company Finance*, Brian Tew and R.F.Henderson, Cambridge 1959, Table 8.1, p109.

13. *ibid.*

14. A.R.Desai, *Social Background of Indian Nationalism*, 3rd ed., Bombay 1959, p99.

15. D.L.Spencer, *India, Mixed Enterprise and Western Business*, The Hague 1959, p 28.

16. Kate Mitchell, *Industrialization of the Western Pacific*, New York 1942, pp284–5.

17. P.A.Wadia & K.T.Merchant, *Our Economic Problems*, 5th ed., cited in A.R.Desai, *Recent Trends in Indian Nationalism*, Bombay 1960, p29.

18. J. Enoch Powell, *Saving in a Free Society*, London 1960, Table II, p29.

19. *Treasury Bulletin for Industry*, no.119, April 1959.

20. S.J.Prais, 'Dividend Policy and Income Appropriation', in *op. cit.* Tew & Henderson, p26.

21. 'The Employment of Savings', *Midland Bank Review*, November 1960, Table, p10.

22. See, for example, the Government White Paper, *Powers of Investment of Trustees in Great Britain*, Cmnd 915, December 1959.

23. Committee on the Working of the Monetary System, *Report*, (Radcliffe Report), Cmnd 827, 1959, p90.

24. *Barclays Bank Review* inset, February 1961.

25. *Economic Report of the US President*, January 1960, cited in A.Shonfield, *The Attack on World Poverty*, London, 1960, p176.

26. K.S.Karol, 'A View of de Gaulle's France', *New Statesman*, 17 February, 1961, p249.

27. *Raw Materials in the US Economy*, *Working Paper no. 1*, Washington DC: US Department of Commerce, Bureau of the Census, 1954, cited in *World Economic Survey 1955*, p36n.

28. See Chapter 6 in this volume.

29. The lower is an official estimate for 1953–59 in *Assistance from the United Kingdom for Overseas Development*, Cmnd 974, 1960, p6; the higher is A.R.Conan's estimate for 1956–57 in *Capital Imports into Sterling Countries*, London 1960, p84.

30. Between 1885 and 1895 capital exports from Britain averaged some £30 million a year, between 1895 and 1905 – some £40 million a year, or, in terms of today's prices, about £100 million a year over the whole period. It was only between 1905 and 1913 that capital exports were heavy – some £200 million a year – but even then they did not reach the £150 million mark – roughly the current level in real terms – until 1910 (See discussion and sources in Conan, *op. cit.*, p82.) Herbert Feis estimates a 1910–13 annual average of £185 million (*Europe the World's Banker, 1870–1914*, Yale, 1931, pp14–5).

31. A very rough estimate based on Feis, *op. cit.*, p5.

32. Roughly calculated from the estimates given in the text and the Blue Books on *National Income and Expenditure*.

33. Feis, *op. cit.* pp5, 14–5.

34. Sources as in note 31.

35. Feis, *op. cit.*, p16; a figure of 20 per cent for 1914 is given by L.H.Jenks in *The Migration of British Capital to 1875*, London 1938, pp5–6.

36. Annual average of 'net income from abroad' for 1953–56 as given in the Blue Books plus an estimated £200 million in profit retentions abroad as given in *The Times* (24 April 1958).

37. A.R.Hall, 'A Note on the English Capital Market as a Source of Funds for Home Investment before 1914', *Economica*, February 1957, p62.

38. *The International Flow of Private Capital 1956–1958*, New York: United Nations 1959, p51.

39. Conan, *op. cit.*, p49.

40. *ibid.*, p50.

41. *ibid.*, p64.

42. *Foreign Aid Program, compilation of studies and surveys*, US Senate, Special Committee to Study the Foreign Aid Program, Study no.7, 85th Congress, 1st Session, 1957, p2.

43. Conan, *op. cit.*, p50.

44. This is a conservative figure based on the *Statist's* 1939 estimate for British private investment of Rs930 crores and the RBI *Census* count for mid-1948 of Rs320 crores of which 72 per cent – or Rs230 crores – was British. Even if the *Statist* figures are halved to account for Indian capital wrongly smuggled in, at least half the pre-war total must have been withdrawn. The withdrawal became a panic after the August 1942 'days' of nationalist uprising.

45. Based on RBI *Census* Tables III-27, III-28; RBI *Bulletin*, Vol. XII no.9, Table 3, p1010.

46. Jocelyn G. Clark in a paper read to 'The International Conference', Ghent, Summer 1959.

47. Mammon in the *Observer*, 23 April 1961.

48. The *Guardian* (25 April 1961) reported the General Secretary's reply to the main political debate in these terms: 'Mr Ghosh was emphatic that a national democratic front could not be built by ignoring the Congress Party. He made it clear that the object of the front was not to overthrow the Congress Government or to take the country along the path of non-capitalist development but for democratic reforms and for defending and strengthening all that is progressive in the Government's policies.'

8. Memories of Development

The economic development of backward countries became a problem in western analysis only after the second world war, some time after it had emerged as a problem in practice. Until then the future seemed well taken care of: capitalism would reach into the outermost bounds of the earth in search of raw materials and trade outlets. It would sap the self-sufficiency of the local economies wherever it went, and would draw them into systematic contact with the world market.

On occasion, it would be bloody, and civilized men guarding the uncertain marches between purposive violence and brutality might be shamed. But they would not denounce the system for that alone, for the mission it was pursuing with its boots was a civilizing one, *absolutely* in the canon of the classical political economists, *relatively* in Marx. It was bringing to the entire world the benign influence of capitalism's superior productivity and leading mankind to a common heritage.

These civilized men were wrong, and by the mid to late 'forties they were said to be wrong, not only by the marxist and other subcultures of political criticism, but by the main body of academic economists concerned with development.

First published in *New Society*, 4 March 1971.

The capitalist system certainly grew, but not always – not, for instance, during the two world wars and the intervening depression. It did wrench the backward countries into alignment with the world market, but it also stopped them from fully entering it.

The cheap materials that poured out of the modern mining and plantation enclaves in backward countries did encourage further specialization downstream – in the capitalist heartlands. The demand for equipment, skills and services for use in these enclaves did the same upstream – again, 'at home,' not in the host environment. The size of investment, the scale of operation, the experience of social control, all swelled where capitalism was already a going concern.

But everywhere else, indigenous society subsided into increasing agriculturalization and unemployment, a loss of skills and productivity – a spiral of growing backwardness and poverty. Growing futility, too, since the invasion of capitalism had both destroyed the backward countries' social and economic integration, and raised the price of entry into the new system beyond their immediate reach.

So, by the end of the 'forties, the academic mainstream had turned interventionist, almost to a man. Academics prescribed, planned, travelled tirelessly, in the cause of policy. They advised governments to harness to domestic 'take-off' the development impulses leaking abroad; they pressed for large initial efforts and therefore for state planning and state enterprise; they masterminded a protracted war on the theory and practice of economic liberalism.

They were not agreed on everything. They quarrelled about the extent to which the backward countries could, or should, be protected in the initial stages of their development; the place for foreign capital; the best use of aid; the relative merits of state and private enterprise. More recently a cocky neo-liberal minority has struck out alone, impressed by the seemingly irrepressible growth of world trade and the obvious failure of their colleagues.

But, by and large, the postwar orthodoxy has survived. For each country, it goes, there is a pattern of production that would both employ its people, and be reasonably efficient in world terms; governments should create that pattern, alone or with outside help. It is the optimistic, interventionist orthodoxy, enshrined in McNamara's World Bank, which only last month denied promised funds to Gabon for not having exercised sufficient control over the foreign interests despoiling that country's resources.

There is an eastern orthodoxy as well. It too has undergone change, although in an opposite direction. As it emerged from the intense Russian debate on industrialization in the mid-twenties, it totally opposed all thought of development through integration with the ruling system of production and trade. On the contrary, if Russia was to avoid military defeat or economic suffocation, or both, at the hands of that system, she would have to withdraw as far as possible from contact with it, exercise the strictest control over what little remained of foreign trade, and pour everything into a huge, broadbased industrialization. Implicit in the approach, although not expressed at the time, was the idea that the planned economy would ultimately prove its superiority by winning for Russian industry a place in the world system on Russian terms – that is, as part of an integrated, articulated and developed national economy.

Long before that stage was reached, however, the early orthodoxy had foundered. The eastern Europeans rose against its terrible cost in the mid-fifties and won a mite of freedom. A second round is being fought out now. Within Russia herself, the threat of economic rundown is impelling the government to open the country more and more to world trade, including trade with the backward countries. And the economists have been forced to rediscover, and commend, the advantages of an international division of labour – the 'dynamic comparative advantage' of western economics.

The new eastern orthodoxy on development is not like its western counterpart in all respects. It is more interventionist, more autarkist, more state-capitalist. It deals in longer time spans and larger scale. It is slightly less crippled by academic casuistry, and slightly more by political and social constraints. But it does share the basic assumption of the major western school – that development is possible in the world we know: that there is something the backward countries themselves can do, with or without outside help, some trick of policy, that can shift the world pattern of production and distribution in their favour, so that they might be absorbed into it as whole societies.

The reality is harsher than that. The minimum cost of entry into the world market is growing every day. The resources from which to fund it in backward countries are not. The relative size of this critical minimum – made up of a minimum development effort (in investment, distribution, education, government, ideology and so on), and the minimum defence effort on which it is predicated – is the nub of the problem of underdevelopment. Take China, the plain man's best example of a country that can 'make it'; which has the resources, the discipline, the leadership – the everything – needed to impose its own amendments on the world; which has already made remarkable material progress since the communists took over.

China also makes nuclear weapons, and the missiles to deliver them. Abhorrent as these are from a socialist or simply humanitarian standpoint, they do make sense in terms of national interest and nationalist ideology, as well as in narrow military terms. Technologically, they are obviously an amazing achievement. But from the point of view of economic and social development they are a disaster.

The claim has not yet been made that Mao's thoughts are especially effective in smashing atoms, so we can presume that

China's scientists, many of whom were trained abroad, use techniques similar to those used in the rest of the world, and need resources of a roughly similar order of magnitude. For example, it seems reasonable to suppose that they use as much electricity in the production of fissile material as the Americans used in their first gas diffusion plant at Oak Ridge, Tennessee – some 14·9 billion kilowatt hours a year or *one quarter, to one half, of total Chinese electricity production in 1964* – depending on whether one accepts Russian or American figures. The Chinese might be using a like proportion of scientists, technicians and skilled workers; of scarce materials, services and components. Even if they are not, even if they enjoy all the advantages of late-coming, and do not have to pull skilled workers out of the armed forces, or empty their Treasury of silver, or requisition men and machines from other urgent uses, as the Americans did thirty years ago, they must still be diverting a huge proportion of their productive capacity from productive use.

This is not something they can afford to do. The critical minimum development effort is growing as violently as the military one. When Mao took power, a four to five million ton/year steel plant was exceptional, a one to two million ton/year plant large. Now the Japanese are setting a floor to viability at ten to twelve million tons a year. Of course, Chinese steel can be, and is, protected; and so is every single branch of Chinese production.

But the economy as a whole is not, and cannot be. Ultimately, it will have to prove its viability in competition with the rest of the world – economically, if possible, militarily if need be. Or collapse.

The scale of the effort needed makes it unlikely that the proof will be forthcoming. Given the alternative, it must be tried. So the Great Leap Forward is followed by the Cultural Revolution, and the Cultural Revolution will no doubt be followed by another gigantic social spasm, and that by another, as the ineluctable necessity to achieve a given initial size pushes the Chinese regime to the limit in gathering and deploying the economic surplus, and to even greater extremes in centralizing the political and social authority to make that possible. All this, while propounding devolution and mass involvement.

But there are limits beyond which they dare not step. Once the unity of the country and the continued coherence of the state are called into question, centralization must necessarily stop.

And if that happens before it can produce the critical minima, development itself becomes a dream. China's fate is not an internal Chinese matter. Failure is bound to close the period in which a Russian-type state capitalist development could be thought feasible for backward countries, even if the more orthodox western variant was not; in which the bloody, treacherous forced march through autarkic industrialization could be thought to constitute progress in some restricted sense; in which the west could find it expedient to temper its savagery here and there, in order to offset the attraction of this 'progress'.

Above all, failure means the end of a terrible illusion, held as fervently by many seeming revolutionaries as by members of the more orthodox schools: that economic development in backward countries is possible without revolution in the developed; that there is hope of a humane existence for the majority of mankind while the Russo-American system of conflict continues to generate its frightful military and economic pressure waves.

Real optimism hangs on the death of that illusion.

List of works cited

Amin, Samir. *L'accumulation à l'échelle mondiale*, Paris: Editions Anthropos 1971.

Atkinson, A.B. 'Who are the Poorest ?' *New Society*, 1 March 1973.

Baran, Paul A. and Sweezy, Paul M. *Monopoly Capital*, New York and London: Monthly Review Press 1966.

Barclays Bank Review. London, quarterly.

Bell, Phillip W. *The Sterling Area in the Postwar World*, Oxford: Clarendon Press 1956.

Bernstein, Eduard. 'On the Meaning of the Marxist Theory of Value' in *Evolutionary Socialism*, London: ILP 1909.

Böhm-Bawerk, Eugen von. *Karl Marx and the Close of his System*, and Rudolf Hilferding, *Böhm-Bawerk's Criticism of Marx*, edited with an introduction by Sweezy, Paul M., New York: Augustus M. Kelly 1949.

Bortkiewicz, Ladislaus von. 'On the Correction of Marx's Fundamental Theoretical Construction in the Third Volume of *Capital*', 1907, translated and introduced by Paul M. Sweezy in Böhm-Bawerk and Hilferding *loc. cit.*

The Brain Drain From Five Developing Countries, UNITAR Research Report no.5, 1971.

Cochran, S. and Eldridge, D.P. 'Employment and Personal Consumption Expenditures', *Monthly Labor Review*, March 1972.

Conan, A.R. *Capital Imports into Sterling Countries*, London: Macmillan 1960.

Construction Review. US Department of Commerce, Bureau of Domestic Commerce.

Consumers Buying Indicators. US Department of Commerce, Series P-65, no.35, May 1971.

Desai, A.R. *Recent Trends in Indian Nationalism*, Bombay: Popular Book Depot 1960.

Desai, A.R. *Social Background of Indian Nationalism*, 3rd ed., Bombay: Popular Book Depot 1959.

Dresch, Stephen P. *Disarmament: Economic Consequences and Developmental Potential*, United Nations Department of Economic and Social Affairs, Centre for Development Planning, Projections and Policies, December 1972 (cyclostyled).

The Economist. London, weekly.

Economic Report of the US President. Washington DC, annual.

Emmanuel, Arghiri. *Unequal Exchange. A Study of the Imperialism of Trade*, London: New Left Books 1972.

Emmanuel, Arghiri. 'White-Settler Colonialism and the Myth of Investment Imperialism', *New Left Review* 73, May–June 1972.

Feis, Herbert. *Europe the World's Banker 1870–1914*, Yale University Press for the Council on Foreign Relations 1931.

Florence, P. Sargant. *Ownership, Control and Success of Large Companies*, London: Sweet and Maxwell 1961.

Fortune Magazine. Chicago, monthly.

Galbraith, John Kenneth. *The Affluent Society*, Penguin 1962.

Gokhale Institute of Politics and Economics. *Notes on the Rise of the Business Communities in India*, New York: Institute of Pacific Relations, 1951 (cyclostyled).

Government of India. Cabinet Secretariat. *National Sample Survey*, Delhi.

Government of India. Central Statistical Office. *Brochure on Revised Series of National Product for 1960–61 to 1964–65,* New Delhi, 1967.

Government of India. Central Statistical Organization. *Annual Survey of Industries,* Calcutta.

Government of India. *Economic Survey,* Delhi.

Government of India. *Defence Service Estimates,* Delhi.

Government of India. Ministry of Labour and Employment. *Tripartite Conclusions 1942–1962,* Delhi, 1962.

Government of India. Planning Commission. *Fourth Five Year Plan, a draft outline,* New Delhi, 1966.

Hall, A. R. 'A Note on the English Capital Market as a Source of Funds for Home Investment before 1914', *Economica,* February, 1957.

Harris, Nigel and Palmer, John (eds). *World Crisis. Essays in Revolutionary Socialism,* London: Hutchinson 1971.

Harrison, John. 'The Political Economy of Housework', *Bulletin of the Conference of Socialist Economists,* Winter 1973.

Harrison, John. 'Productive and Unproductive Labour in Marx's Political Economy', *Bulletin of the Conference of Socialist Economists,* Autumn 1973.

Healey, J. M. 'Industrialization, Capital Intensity and Efficiency', *Oxford Institute of Economics and Statistics Bulletin,* November 1968.

Henderson, G. 'Emigration of Highly Skilled Manpower from the Developing Countries', UNITAR Research Report no.3, 1970.

Hilferding, Rudolf. *Böhm-Bawerk's Criticism of Marx,* in Böhm-Bawerk, see above.

India. Central Statistical Office. *Brochure on Revised Series of National Product for 1960–61 to 1964–65,* n.p. [New Delhi], 1967.

India. *Economic Survey,* New Delhi, annual.

India. Labour Bureau. Ministry of Labour and Employment. *Indian Labour Statistics,* Simla.

MCT

India. Ministry of Labour and Employment. *Tripartite Conclusions 1942-1962*, New Delhi, 1962.

India. Planning Commission. *Fourth Five Year Plan, a draft outline*, New Delhi, 1966.

India. The Statistical Section, Coffee Board. *Coffee Statistics*, Bangalore: The Secretary, Coffee Board.

Indian Labour Journal. Simla, monthly.

Indian Labour Yearbook. Simla, annual.

International Labour Office. *Yearbook of Labour Statistics*, Geneva, annual.

Jeffereys, James B. and Walters, Dorothy. 'National Income and Expenditure of the United Kingdom, 1870-1952' in Simon Kuznets (ed), *Income and Wealth*, Series V, London: Bowes & Bowes 1955.

Jenks, Leland H. *The Migration of British Capital to 1875*, London: Jonathan Cape 1938.

Karol, K. S. 'A View of de Gaulle's France', *New Statesman* 17 February 1961.

Kidron, Michael. 'Reform and Revolution', *International Socialism* 7, Winter 1961-62.

Kidron, Michael. *Foreign Investments in India*, London: Oxford University Press 1965.

Kitzinger, U. V. *The Challenge of the Common Market*, Oxford: Basil Blackwell 1961.

Liesner, H. H. *The Import Dependence of Britain and Western Germany*, Princeton, NJ: Princeton Studies in International Finance, no.7, 1957.

Lenin, Vladimir Ilyich. *Collected Works*, Moscow, 1960 *et seq*.

Maizels, Alfred. *Industrial Growth and World Trade*, Cambridge University Press 1963.

Mandel, Ernest. *Traité d'économie marxiste*, Paris: Julliard 1962; translated by Brian Pearce as *Marxist Economic Theory*, London: Merlin Press 1968.

Marx Karl. *A Contribution to the Critique of Political Economy*, Calcutta: Bharati Library (nd).

Marx, Karl. *Capital*, Moscow: Foreign Languages Publishing House, 1961 *et seq.*

Marx, Karl. *Theories of Surplus Value*, Moscow: Foreign Languages Publishing House (nd).

Mattick, Paul. *Marx and Keynes*, Boston: Extending Horizons Books 1969.

Meek, Ronald L. *Studies in the Labour Theory of Value*, London: Lawrence & Wishart 1956.

Meek, Ronald L. 'Some Notes on the "Transformation Problem" ', reprinted in *Economics and Ideology and other Essays*, London: Chapman & Hall 1967.

Midland Bank Review. London, quarterly.

Mitchell, Kate. *Industralization of the Western Pacific*, New York: Institute of Pacific Relations 1942.

Monthly Labour Review. Washington DC, December 1971.

Morgenstern, Oskar. *The Question of National Defense*, 2nd rev. ed., New York: Vintage Books 1961.

New Society, London, weekly.

Nicholson, R. J. 'Capital Stock, Employment and Output in British Industry 1948–1964,' *Yorkshire Bulletin of Economic and Social Research*, November 1966.

Palloix, Christian. 'The Question of Unequal Exchange: A Critique of Political Economy', *Bulletin of the Conference of Socialist Economists*, 2, 1 Spring 1972.

Pardiwalla, J. J. 'Exchange Banks in India', Bombay University, PhD thesis 1950 (typescript).

Pejovich, Svetozar. *The Market-Planned Economy of Yugoslavia*, Minneapolis: University of Minnesota Press 1966.

Phillips, Joseph D. 'Estimating the Economic Surplus', in Baran and Sweezy, *loc. cit.*

Pilling, Geoff. 'Political Economy and Imperialism: the Work of Arghiri Emmanuel', *Economy and Society*, Vol. 2 no.2, May 1973.

Powell, J. Enoch. *Saving in a Free Society*, London: Hutchinson for The Institute of Economic Affairs 1960.

Prais, S. J. 'Dividend Policy and Income Appropriation', in Tew & Henderson, *op. cit.*

Primoff, Charles. 'Balancing Resource Requirements Against Resource Capabilities', in Yoshpe, Harry B. (ed), *loc. cit.*

Problems of International Investment. London: Royal Institute of International Affairs 1938.

Robinson, E.A.G., and Kidron, Michael (eds), *Economic Development in South Asia*, London: MacMillan, New York: St Martin's Press, 1970.

Robinson, Joan. *Economic Philosophy*, Penguin 1964.

(Radcliffe) Committee on the Working of the Monetary System. *Report*, London: HMSO August 1959 (Cmnd 827).

Reserve Bank of India. *Bulletin*, Bombay, monthly.

Routh, Guy. *Occupation and Pay in Great Britain, 1906–1960*, Cambridge University Press 1965.

Schlesinger, Rudolph. *Marx, His Time and Ours*, London: Routledge and Kegan Paul 1950.

Shonfield, Andrew. *The Attack on World Poverty*, London: Chatto and Windus 1960.

Socialist Worker. London, weekly.

Soltow, A. (ed). *Six Papers on the Size Distribution of Wealth and Income*, New York: National Bureau of Economic Research 1969.

Spencer, D. L. *India, Mixed Enterprise and Western Business*, The Hague: Martinus Nijhoff 1959.

Sraffa, Piero. *Production of Commodities by Means of Commodities*, Cambridge University Press 1960.

The Statist. London, weekly until 1967.

Stockholm International Peace Research Institute. *World Armaments and Disarmament*, Stockholm: Almquist and Wiksell, annual.

Stockholm International Peace Research Institute. *The Arms*

Trade with the Third World, Stockholm: Almqvist and Wiksell 1971.

Strachey, John. *The End of Empire*, London: Gollancz 1959.

Survey of Current Business. Washington DC.

Sweezy, Paul M. *The Theory of Capitalist Development*, London: Dennis Dobson 1946.

Tea Board of India. *Tea Statistics*, Calcutta Tea Board.

Tew, Brian and Henderson, R. F. *Studies in Company Finance*, London: Cambridge University Press 1959.

Thorner, Daniel. *Investment in Empire*, Philadelphia, Pennsylvania University Press 1950.

UNESCO: *Statistical Yearbook*, annual.

United Kingdom. Central Statistical Office. *Social Trends*, London, HMSO.

United Kingdom. *Defence Estimates* (Army), annual.

United Kingdom. *Powers of Investment of Trustees in Great Britain*, Cmnd 915, December 1959.

United Kingdom. Central Statistical Office. *Annual Abstract of Statistics*, London: HMSO, annual.

United Kingdom. Central Statistical Office. *National Income and Expenditure*, London: HMSO, annual.

United Kingdom. *Assistance from the United Kingdom for Overseas Development*, Cmnd 974, March 1960.

United Kingdom. Board of Trade. *Economic Trends*, monthly.

United Kingdom. *Bulletin for Industry*.

United Nations. *Economic Development of Under-Developed Countries, Relative Prices of Primary Products and Manufacturers in International Trade*, New York, 1953.

United Nations. *The International Flow of Private Capital 1946–1952*, New York, 1954.

United Nations. *The International Flow of Private Capital, 1956–1958*, New York, 1959.

United Nations. *Measures for the Economic Development of Under-Developed Countries*, New York, 1951.

United Nations. *World Economic Survey*, New York, annual.

US Census of Population 1960, Washington: Department of Commerce.

United States. Bureau of Labor Statistics. *Survey of Consumer Income and Expenditure for 1960–61* (BLS Report no.237–93), Washington, DC:US GPO February 1965.

United States. Department of Commerce. Bureau of the Census; *Raw Materials in the United States Economy*, Working Paper no.7, Washington DC, 1954.

United States. House of Representatives. Committee on Government Operations, Research and Technical Programs Subcommittee. *Hearings on The Brain Drain of Scientists, Engineers and Physicians from the Developing Countries to the US*, 90th Congress, Second Session, 23 January 1968.

United States, Joint Economic Committee of the US Congress, Sub-Committee on Foreign Economic Policy. *New Directions in the Soviet Economy*, Washington DC, 1966.

United States. Senate. Special Committee to Study the Foreign Aid Program. *Foreign Aid Program, compilation of studies and surveys*, Study no.7, 85th Congress, 1st session, Washington DC, 1957.

Vernon, Raymond. *Sovereignty at Bay*, New York and London: Basic Books 1971.

Watanabe, S. 'The Brain Drain from Developing to Developed Countries', *International Labour Review*, April 1969.

Yoshpe, Harry B., Franke, Charles F. *et al.*; *Production for Defence*, Washington DC: Industrial College of the Armed Forces, 1968.

Yoshpe, Harry B. (ed) *Requirements: Matching Needs with Resources*, Washington DC: Industrial College of the Armed Forces 1964.

Index

The Bolsheviks and the October Revolution

Central Committee Minutes of the Russian Social-Democratic Labour Party (bolsheviks) August 1917–February 1918

Translated from the Russian by Ann Bone

Revolution in Russia, October 1917, meant that posterity was to inherit a new society. What remains is a scrapbook – the notes for the Bolshevik Central Committee, hurriedly pencilled on torn-out sheets of paper.

Captured in these notes is the deep division that lay between revolutionaries and routinists on the central committee, between men terrified to lose and men terrified to grasp the opportunity to change the pace of history.

The minutes are extensively supplemented by documents, the official notes of the Institute of Marxism-Leninism, Moscow, together with additional notes and comments for this edition.

£2.70 paperback   £6.60 hardback

 **Pluto Press, Unit 10 Spencer Court
7 Chalcot Road, London NW1 8LH**

The Hazards of Work: How to Fight Them

Patrick Kinnersly

Patrick Kinnersly wrote *The Hazards of Work* in the belief that bad working conditions needed to be changed not just deplored; and that the people who could best change them were the ones who lived in them and suffered from them. So he wrote *for* workers, not *about* them, and in language that can be understood.

This book soon became a major instrument in the struggle for health and safety at work. It is used directly by workers in improving workshop conditions. Trade unions issue it to their officers. Factory inspectors consult it. Industrial tutors prescribe it. Even managements cannot do without it.

Michael Foot, Secretary of State for Employment, has said of it in the House of Commons: '. . . an excellent book . . . I recommend it to all who are interested in health and safety at work . . . there is certainly a more astringent approach to the subject in *The Hazards of Work* than there is in some parts of the Robens doctrine.' 3 April 1974.

90p paperback   £2.70 hardback

Pluto Press, Unit 10 Spencer Court 7 Chalcot Road, London NW1 8LH